THE
BiG
HUMAN
BODY
ACTIVITY BOOK

Buster Books

ILLUSTRATED BY
RHYS JEFFERYS, GEORGIE FEARNS
AND MARC PATTENDEN

WRITTEN BY BEN ELCOMB
EDITED BY IMOGEN CURRELL-WILLIAMS
AND HELEN BROWN
DESIGNED BY ZOE BRADLEY
COVER DESIGNED BY JOHN BIGWOOD

WITH SPECIAL THANKS TO
DR KRISTINA ROUTH

First published in Great Britain in 2020 by Buster Books, an imprint of
Michael O'Mara Books Limited, 9 Lion Yard, Tremadoc Road, London SW4 7NQ

W www.mombooks.com/buster F Buster Books   @BusterBooks

Copyright © 2020 Buster Books

With additional material adapted from www.shutterstock.com

ISBN: 978-1-78055-632-1

3 5 7 9 10 8 6 4 2

This book was printed in June 2020 by Leo Paper Products Ltd,
Heshan Astros Printing Limited, Xuantan Temple Industrial Zone,
Gulao Town, Heshan City, Guangdong Province, China.

HUMAN BODY PUZZLE FUN

Your body is completely awe-inspiring. It is made up of lots of parts that work together in very clever ways, and all these pieces join together to make one remarkable person: YOU.

This book will take you on an extraordinary journey through the human anatomy, as you challenge yourself with muscle-stretching, brain-boggling puzzles. Alongside the activities are tons of hair-raising facts to help you get right under the skin of your body. Prepare to learn about everything from your muscles and your blood to your germs and your poo.

Some of the words used in this book may be tricky to understand at first. You can ask a family member or friend to explain the meaning of a word or turn to the glossary on pages 127–128. All the scientific words used in this book are listed there, with a brief description of their meaning. The answers to all the puzzles are also at the back of the book on pages 116–126.

Get ready to puzzle – it's time to explore the amazing human body.

JOINING JOINTS

These images are X-rays of different joints. Look at the X-rays and work out which joints they are. Can you match them to the names on the clipboards below?

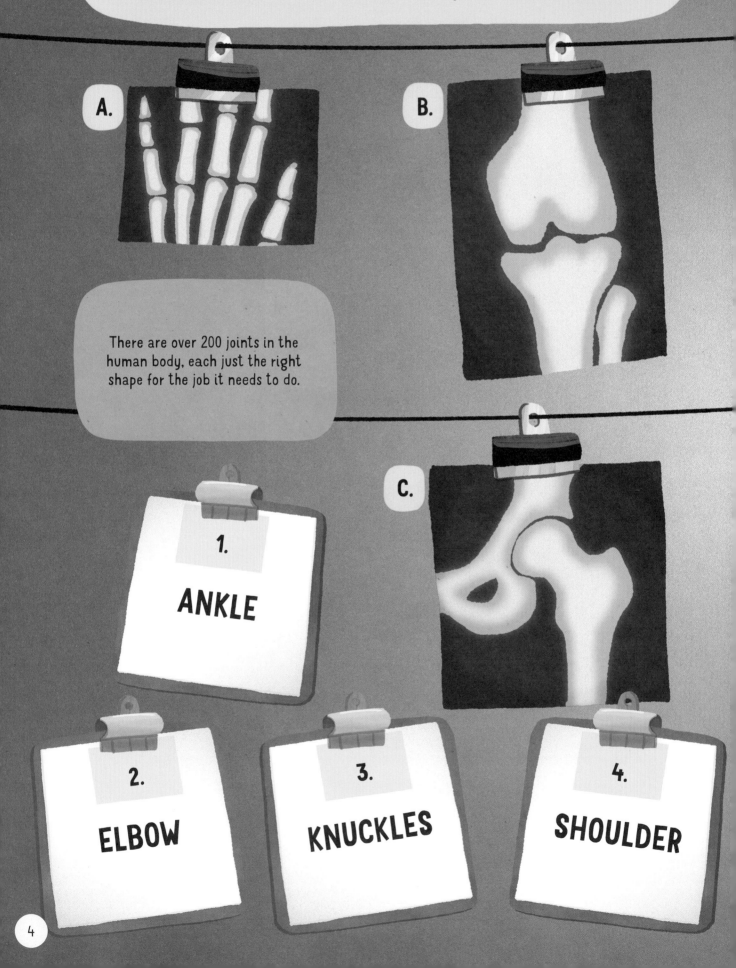

A.

B.

There are over 200 joints in the human body, each just the right shape for the job it needs to do.

C.

1.
ANKLE

2.
ELBOW

3.
KNUCKLES

4.
SHOULDER

D.

E.

Joints that are able to move are called synovial joints. They are mostly located in the arms and legs, where movement is especially important. Some joints, like those in the skull where a solid structure is needed, hold the bones tight against each other and don't let them move.

Have you ever wondered why your joints can sometimes make a cracking noise? The noise occurs when gases build up in the fluid that surrounds the joint. When the joint is stretched, the gases are released quickly and that makes the **POP!**

F.

G.

5.
WRIST

6.
KNEE

7.
HIP

BACTERIA HUNT

How many green bacteria can you find
hiding amongst the white blood cells?

KEY

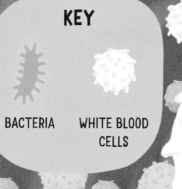

BACTERIA

WHITE BLOOD
CELLS

White blood cells help to defend
the body against infection and
disease. They can engulf
and destroy bacteria.

There can be up to 25,000
white blood cells in a
single drop of blood.

Some white blood cells only
live for a few hours, while
others live for several years.

SUPERHUMAN BODY PARTS

Circle the group below that contains all of the parts you need to make this prosthetic leg.

Prosthetics are artificial replacements for people who are missing a part of their body. It is believed that the first prosthetic was a big toe made for an Egyptian noblewoman.

Running blades are special prosthetics created for athletes. The blades store kinetic (movement) energy in the same way as a spring, allowing athletes to run and jump. The running blades are lighter than a bag of sugar but stronger than steel.

A.

B.

C.

D.

SUPERMARKET SWEEP

Your digestive system, including your stomach and intestines, breaks down food to release essential nutrients. These are then absorbed into the bloodstream. Find the correct path through the supermarket by only collecting the nutrients listed in the key below. Watch out for shoppers blocking your path! How many items are in your basket at the finish?

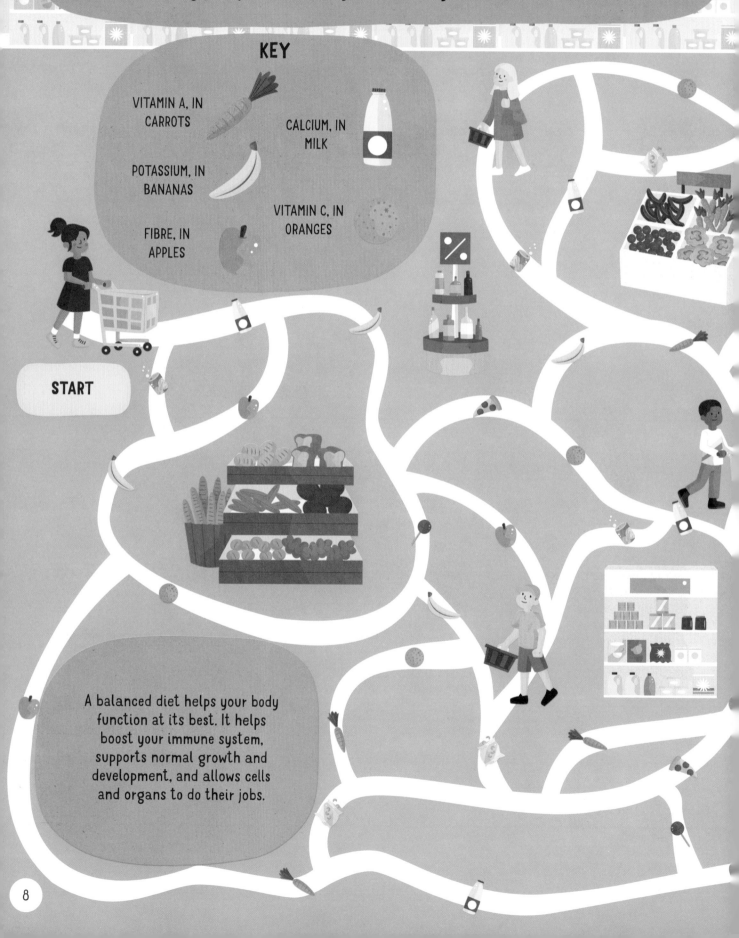

KEY

VITAMIN A, IN CARROTS

CALCIUM, IN MILK

POTASSIUM, IN BANANAS

VITAMIN C, IN ORANGES

FIBRE, IN APPLES

START

A balanced diet helps your body function at its best. It helps boost your immune system, supports normal growth and development, and allows cells and organs to do their jobs.

Use the spaces below to write down how many
of each item you found along the way.

EXIT

MILK	BANANAS	APPLES	ORANGES	CARROTS	TOTAL

FINISH

You can get the nutrients
your body needs by eating
a varied diet. This includes
grain products (brown rice,
barley), vegetables, fruits, milk
and milk products, protein-rich
plant foods (beans, nuts) and
protein-rich animal foods (lean
meat, poultry, fish and eggs).

DECIBEL DISCOVERY

Noise is measured in units called decibels. Follow the tangled lines to work out how many decibels each of the sounds below make.

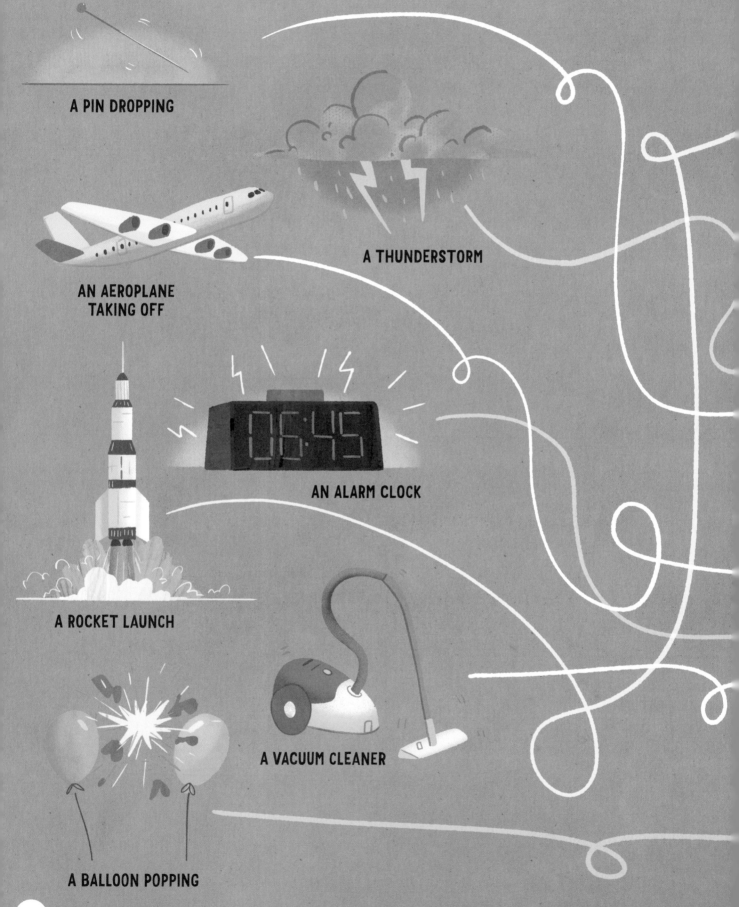

A PIN DROPPING

A THUNDERSTORM

AN AEROPLANE
TAKING OFF

AN ALARM CLOCK

A ROCKET LAUNCH

A VACUUM CLEANER

A BALLOON POPPING

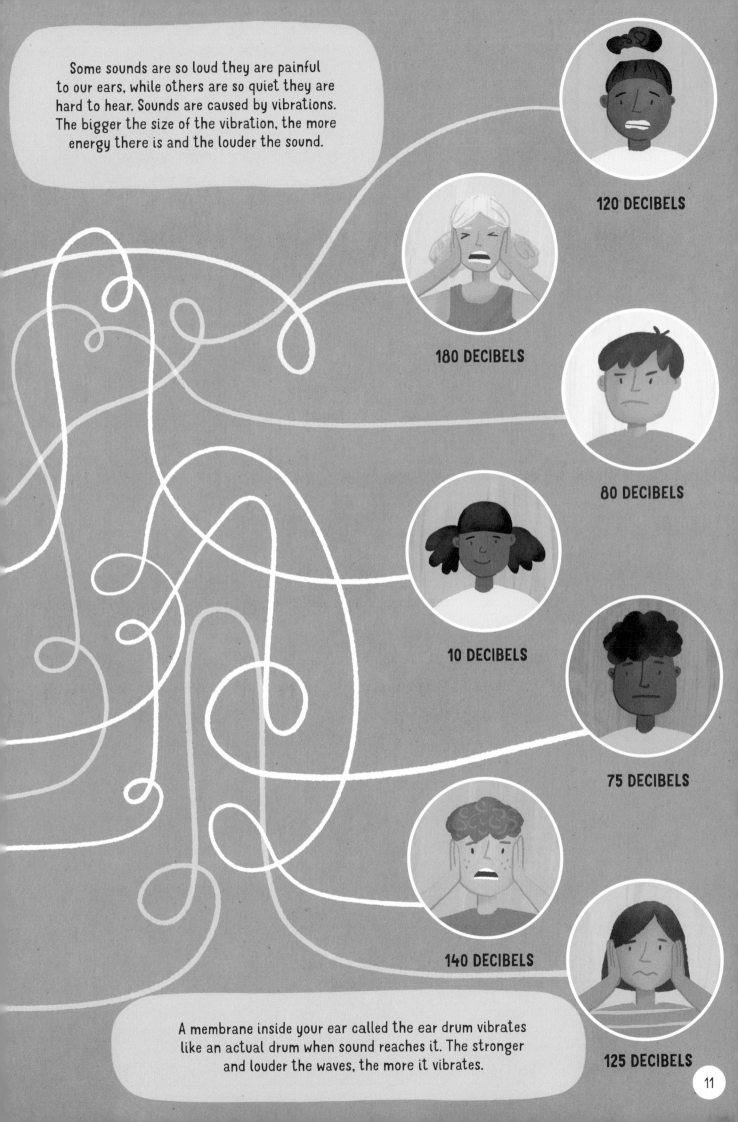

Some sounds are so loud they are painful to our ears, while others are so quiet they are hard to hear. Sounds are caused by vibrations. The bigger the size of the vibration, the more energy there is and the louder the sound.

120 DECIBELS

180 DECIBELS

80 DECIBELS

10 DECIBELS

75 DECIBELS

140 DECIBELS

A membrane inside your ear called the ear drum vibrates like an actual drum when sound reaches it. The stronger and louder the waves, the more it vibrates.

125 DECIBELS

MEDICAL MEMORY MUDDLE (PART ONE)

This museum has an exhibition of medical marvels on display. These are medicines, treatments and scientific discoveries that have been uncovered throughout history. Study the medical discoveries for one minute, then turn over the page and see how many of their names you can remember.

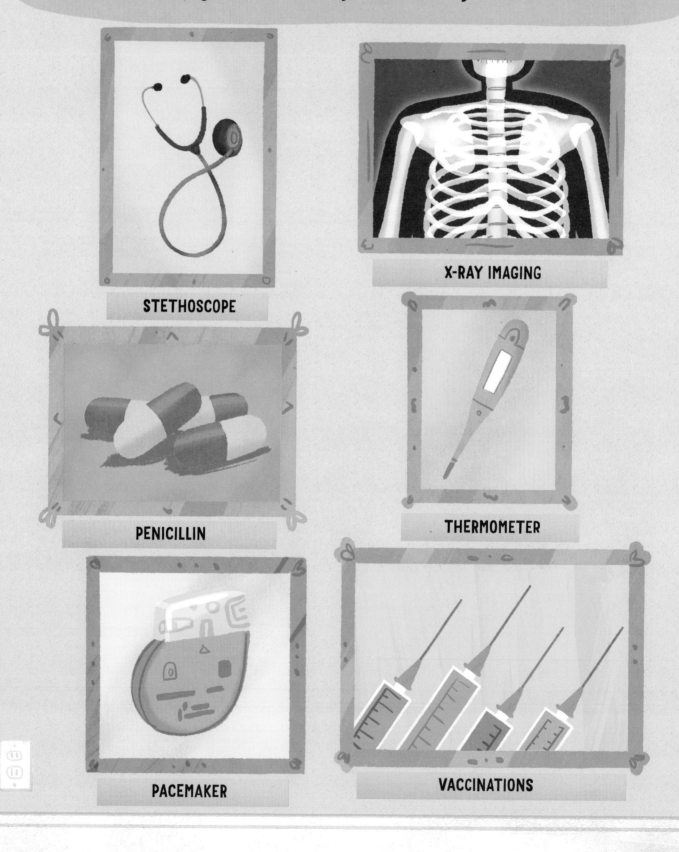

STETHOSCOPE

X-RAY IMAGING

PENICILLIN

THERMOMETER

PACEMAKER

VACCINATIONS

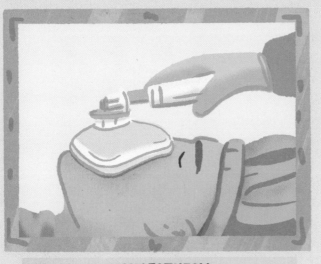

ANAESTHESIA

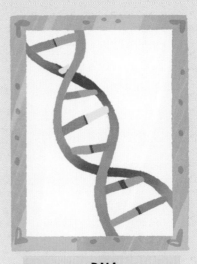

DNA

In 1895, a German physicist called Wilhelm Röntgen used X-radiation to see what was going on inside our bodies. The first X-rays Wilhelm took were of metal objects and his wife's hands.

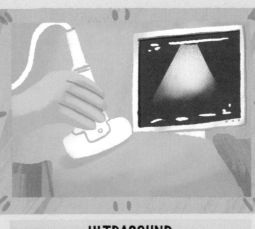

BLOOD GROUPS

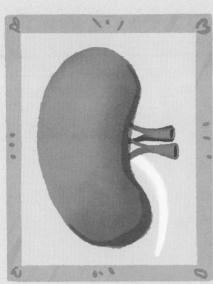

KIDNEY TRANSPLANT

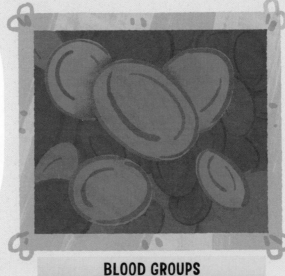

ULTRASOUND

EPIPEN

Ultrasound creates 3D images by beaming high-pitched sound waves into the body. These waves bounce off tissues, creating echoes that a computer turns into images.

MEDICAL MEMORY MUDDLE (PART TWO)

Write the names of as many discoveries as possible underneath their pictures.
Try to remember as much as you can without peeking at the previous pages.

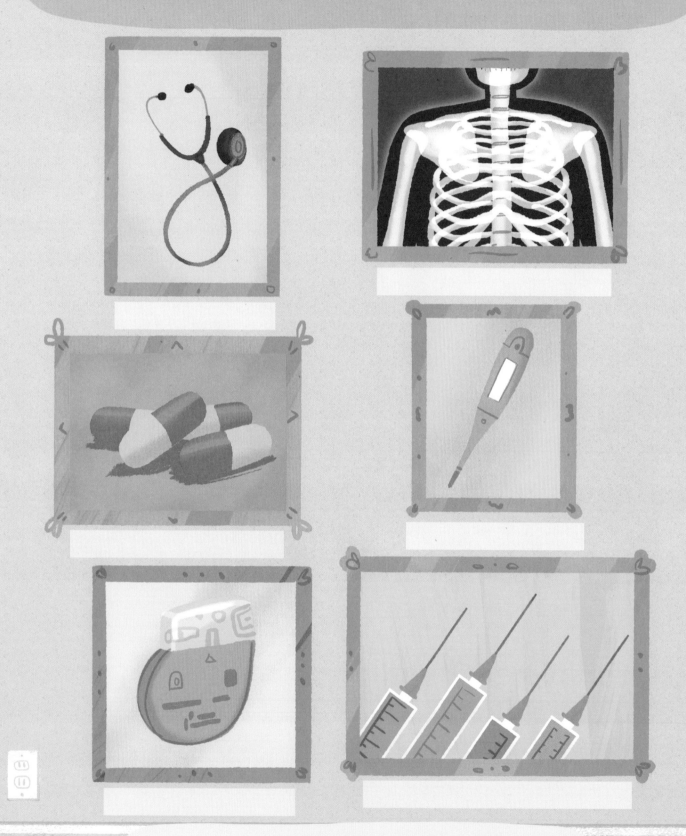

If you unravelled all the DNA in your body, it would
stretch to the moon and back 1,500 times ... or, to put
it another way, to the sun and back four times!

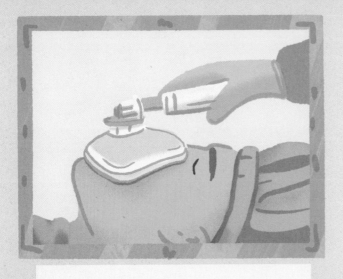

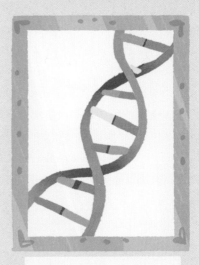

Your heart's sinus node (located in the upper-right chamber of the heart) is your natural pacemaker. It sends an electrical impulse to make your heart beat. First used in the 1950s, a pacemaker is designed to take over the role of your sinus node if it isn't working properly.

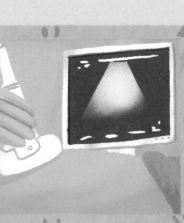

BONUS QUESTION
One picture has changed – can you work out which one?

PERSONALITY FLOW CHART

What kind of person are you — are you a quiet bookworm or the centre of attention? Are you friendly or argumentative? Everyone has a unique personality, which is formed by your genes and your upbringing. Use this simple test to reveal more about your personality.

YES

NO

Do you like doing things that are a bit dangerous?

NO

Do you think others would describe you as shy?

YES

Do you get bored easily with new hobbies and keep starting new ones?

YES

NO

YES

Do you like exploring unfamiliar places?

START

NO

YES

Are you scared of what other people might think of you?

YES

Are you sensitive to criticism?

NO

NO

Do you like to be organized?

YES

NO

Extroverts are energized by being around people and are very sociable. They enjoy exciting, sometimes dangerous, things and are good at doing more than one activity at a time.

Thinkers use logic to make decisions. They will weigh up the pros and cons of trying a new or dangerous thing. They like people who are honest and fair.

Perceivers prefer to keep their options open. They often get bored easily with new hobbies and like to be flexible when making plans with friends.

Introverts often work alone or in small groups. They are sometimes described as shy as they prefer a quieter, slower pace of life.

Feelers are sensitive to negative comments. They think about other people and make decisions based on how others will be affected by their actions.

Sensors are very realistic and they like to focus on the facts and details. They apply common sense to past experiences to come up with practical solutions to problems.

Judgers tend to be organized and prepared. They like to make and stick to plans, and are comfortable following the rules.

Intuitives prefer to focus on feelings and instincts. They are very creative and rely on their imagination and ideas, and like to live in the moment.

WHO POOED?

When you press the flush button, water, toilet paper, your wee and poo go down a pipe called a sewer. Can you follow the sewage pipes to find out which child did the poo?

RAJ

LEO

Although poo might smell bad, this is completely normal. As the food is broken down in your digestive system, it releases a lot of gas and smelly chemicals.

If you don't drink enough water, your body and your poo will be dehydrated. This can make it hard to poo, which is called constipation.

NIA

LEYLA

LILY

Healthy poo is made from a diet that is high in fibre, and helped by drinking lots of water. The fibre makes your poo solid and the water makes it glide through your large intestine.

ANIMAL SIBLINGS

Humans have a lot in common with animals as certain genes perform the same functions across the animal kingdom. Read the facts about each animal below and guess which ones are true and which ones are false.

1. 90 per cent of the genes in an Abyssinian domestic cat are the same as in humans.

2. Mantis shrimp see colour in the same way that humans do.

3. Ring-tailed lemurs are omnivores, like humans. They eat meat and plenty of healthy fruit and vegetables.

4. Whales and dolphins live in human-like families and their brains develop in a similar way to those of humans.

In order to survive, animals need air, water, food and shelter (protection from predators and the environment). This is the same for humans. Every living thing has its own way of making sure its basic needs are met.

5. Frogs use the energy in their food to keep themselves warm, like humans.

6. Dogs have evolved to mimic human facial expressions in order to get sympathy and attention.

8. The skin tissue and heart valves of pigs can be used in medicine because they are so similar to those in the human body.

7. Koalas have fingerprints that are almost identical to human fingerprints.

In the past, many humans thought of themselves as the only creatures with emotions, morality and culture. But many scientists now believe that these traits are also found in animals.

GROWING UP

These six children are in a doctor's surgery. They have had their height measured to see how much they have grown since last year. Read the descriptions below and work out the height of each child.

1. Nathan is 2 cm shorter than 150 cm. How tall is Nathan?

2. Kamal is 10 cm shorter than Nathan. How tall is Kamal?

3. If Ava is 4 cm shorter than Vihaan, what is her height?

The tallest person ever recorded was called Robert Wadlow. He was 272 cm tall, which is as tall as an Asian elephant.

4. If Vihaan is 1 cm shorter than Nathan, how tall is Vihaan?

5. Anna and Ava were the same height last year. Ava is now 6 cm taller. How tall is Anna?

6. Marie is 2 cm taller than Anna. How tall is Marie?

SMELLY BINGO

This bedroom is full of smelly items. Search the room for all of the items pictured on the bingo cards on the opposite page. Time yourself to see how quickly you can find them or challenge a friend to a race.

DOG BED	FLOWERS	SPORTS T-SHIRT
ORANGE PEEL	DIRTY SOCK	BANANA SKIN
MUDDY TOWEL	PIZZA BOX	CLEAN LAUNDRY

Humans have around 5 million odour-detecting cells. Dogs have over 220 million of them!

From the outside, it might look like your nose, ears and mouth are separate, but they are actually all connected inside your head.

APPLE CORE	USED PLATE	TOOTHPASTE
MUDDY TRAINERS	DIRTY SOCK	FIZZY DRINK
RUBBISH BIN	HOT CHOCOLATE	LAVENDER PLANT

PICKING SIDES

The brain is divided into two halves. The left side of the brain tends to control logic, such as speaking and writing skills. The right side tends to be more creative and emotional. Can you look at the pictures below and work out which side of the brain controls them?

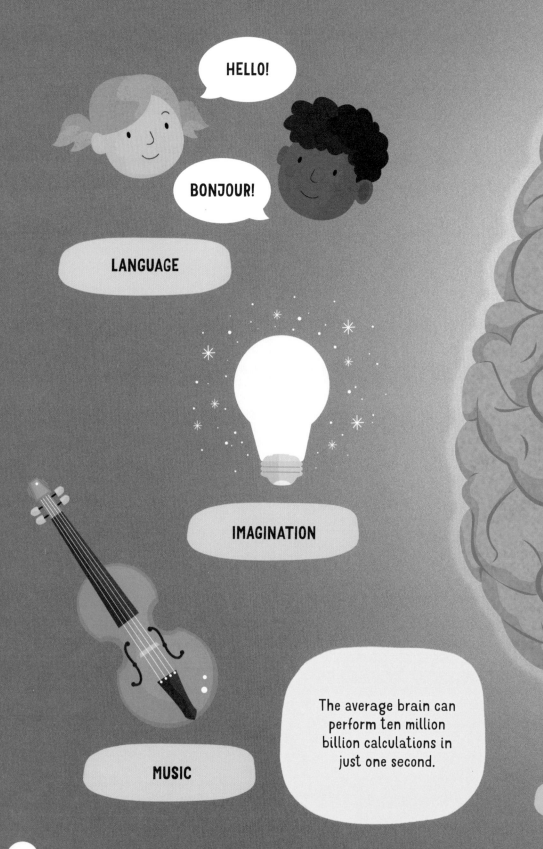

HELLO!

BONJOUR!

LANGUAGE

IMAGINATION

MUSIC

The average brain can perform ten million billion calculations in just one second.

LEFT SIDE

The right side of your brain controls the left side of your body, and the left side of your brain controls the right side of your body.

WRITING

SPATIAL AWARENESS

PUZZLES

MATHS AND SCIENCE

RIGHT SIDE

An adult human brain weighs around 1.4 kg, about the same as nine apples.

ART

SHADOWY SILHOUETTES

Challenge your eyes to the ultimate spotting puzzle.
There are five identical pairs below. Can you find them all?
Draw lines between the silhouettes to pair them up.

Your eye has different cells that help you see in different light levels. Cone cells, for example, help you see colour in bright light.

The pupil is the black hole in the middle of your eye. It gets bigger or smaller depending on the amount of light, so it can stop too much light entering the eye in bright situations.

Rod cells help you see black and white images. They also help you see much better in low light.

STAYING HYDRATED

It's important to consume up to 2,000 ml of liquid every day through food and drink. Each square below contains a mathematical sum that will give you the total amount of liquid in that square. Work out which squares you need to land on to make up 2,000 ml. You can only land on four squares to reach your target.

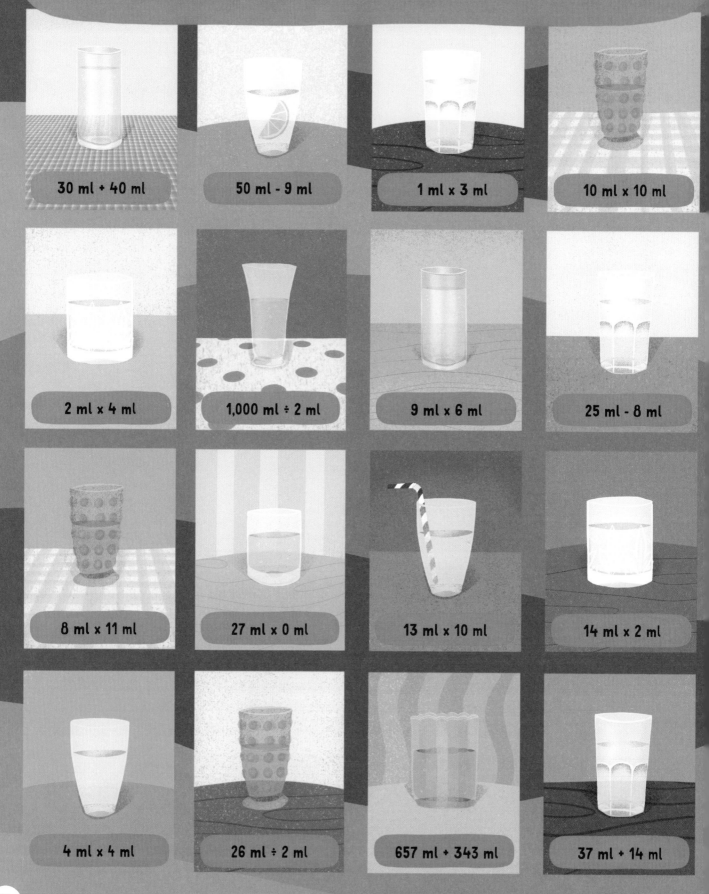

30 ml + 40 ml

50 ml - 9 ml

1 ml x 3 ml

10 ml x 10 ml

2 ml x 4 ml

1,000 ml ÷ 2 ml

9 ml x 6 ml

25 ml - 8 ml

8 ml x 11 ml

27 ml x 0 ml

13 ml x 10 ml

14 ml x 2 ml

4 ml x 4 ml

26 ml ÷ 2 ml

657 ml + 343 ml

37 ml + 14 ml

HEAD SCRATCHING

A head louse is a tiny insect that lives among human hairs and feeds on tiny amounts of blood from the scalp. Nits are the empty egg cases attached to hair that head lice hatch from. Look at the key below and count how many head lice and nits are in this child's hair.

KEY

HEAD LOUSE   NIT

It is estimated that over half of all 11 to 14-year-olds will get head lice every year. But don't worry! You get rid of them with a medicated shampoo and a special, thin comb.

Most people with head lice have an average of 10 to 20 on their head, but there could be more. And these little critters can move fast for their size, at around 23 cm per minute!

Female head lice can live for up to 40 days. Over the course of its life, one head louse can lay up to 100 eggs.

BODY-CLOCK CONUNDRUM

We use clocks to keep us on time each day. But did you know that your body has its own clock? In fact, it has more than one. Look at the clocks below and see if you can work out what time of day matches to the activities on the opposite page.

A. 18:30

B. 22:30

C. 03:00

D. 08:30

G. 02:00

E. 11:00

F. 14:30

H. 16:00

If you've ever been on holiday to a country with a different time zone, you may have found it difficult to go to bed and wake up at your normal time. This is called jet lag. It happens because your body clock is confused.

You have a 24-hour body clock running inside of you. Your body automatically knows when it's time to go to sleep at night or wake up at the start of the day.

1.
MOST LIKELY TO NEED A POO

2.
BEST TIME FOR SPORT

3.
LEAST LIKELY TO NEED A POO

6.
DEEPEST STAGE OF SLEEP

4.
BRAIN FULLY ALERT AND ACTIVE

5.
BLOOD PRESSURE BEGINS TO DROP

8.
LOWEST BODY TEMPERATURE

7.
BEST COORDINATION

REFLEX ROLL

For this game, you will need a counter for each player and a dice. Roll the dice and move your counter clockwise around the board, following the instructions you land on. The winner is the person who gets around the board the most times in five minutes.

You are at the park and a ball is suddenly thrown at you. Your reflex action means your arm raises to try to catch it. Move forward two spaces.

You accidentally put your hand near a hot flame. Your reflex action causes the muscles in your arm to pull your hand out of harm's way. Move forward three spaces.

Reflexes protect your body from things that can cause harm. When you touch something hot, you automatically pull your hand away without really thinking about it. If you fall over, your hands will immediately stretch out to stop your fall.

START

A reflex is an involuntary, or automatic, action that your body does in response to something — without you even having to think about it.

You are cleaning your toothbrush and your tongue with your throat. You push it too far down third of the world population same as one- weak gag reflex. Move back one space.

You are at the doctor's and they tap the area under your kneecap but your lower leg stays still. This might indicate a damage to the nervous system. Move back three spaces.

Many reflexes are caused by your spinal cord sending messages to your muscles without involving the brain. Other reflexes that we do without thinking include blinking, sneezing and yawning.

TOUCH RECEPTORS

Your skin has receptors in it that detect touch. This helps you to react to the environment around you. Look at the pictures below and see if you can match the picture to the correct description at the bottom of the page.

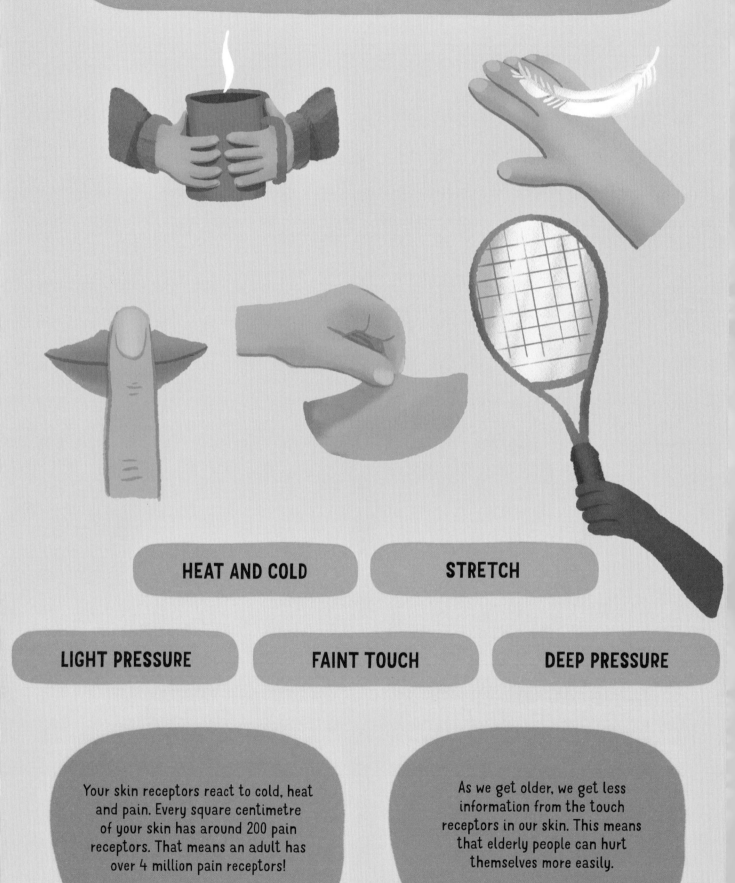

HEAT AND COLD

STRETCH

LIGHT PRESSURE

FAINT TOUCH

DEEP PRESSURE

Your skin receptors react to cold, heat and pain. Every square centimetre of your skin has around 200 pain receptors. That means an adult has over 4 million pain receptors!

As we get older, we get less information from the touch receptors in our skin. This means that elderly people can hurt themselves more easily.

SOLVE THE SUPER SEQUENCE

Can you complete the three mathematical sequences on the strand of DNA?
Figure out what number comes next and write your answers on the dotted lines.

A.

11

14

17

20

....

DNA is short for 'deoxyribonucleic acid'. Each piece of information is carried on a different section of the DNA. These sections are called genes.

There are around 23,000 genes in the human body. This might sound impressive, but a grain of rice has even more.

B.

2

4

8

16

....

DNA is the material that carries all the information about how a living thing will look and function. Among other things, for instance, DNA in humans determines what colour our eyes are.

The International Space Station holds the DNA of a specially selected group of humans, including British scientist Stephen Hawking.

C.

17

19

23

29

....

BODY SWAP

Can you spot ten differences between these two bodies?

The left lung is slightly smaller than the right as it shares space with the heart. Adult lungs breathe in around 9,000 litres of air a day. That's enough air to fill over 100,000 balloons.

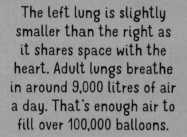

The largest internal organ in the human body is the liver. It is also the heaviest organ, with an average weight of 1.5 kg.

People usually have two kidneys, but can live a normal, healthy life with just one. Your kidneys are found under the ribcage in your back, one on each side of the body. Each adult kidney is about the size of a fist.

WALK THE LINE

Balance is the ability to maintain a controlled body position while performing a task. This skill is used by tightrope walkers who successfully travel along a thin wire. Read the descriptions next to each tightrope walker below and solve the clues to discover where they are trying to go. Then draw a straight line to help them reach the correct destination.

1.

I'm trying to get to the highest platform in our circus tent.

2.

This balancing pole should help me on my journey to the highest point in the city, on top of a glass building.

3.

I want to see the world upside down from my vantage point at the top of a mountain.

4.

I need to reach a cold and icy peak.

5.

I can't see where I'm going, so I have to be careful not to fall in the rushing water when I get there.

6.

I want to find my way to a high brick wall that is nice and flat, so I don't roll away.

Your inner ear contains fluid that helps it send information to your brain about balance. It is this fluid that can make you feel dizzy after you've been spinning around. Your eyes can see that you have stopped, but the fluid in your ears is still moving, leading to a sense of confusion.

A.

B.

C.

Our sense of balance helps to stop us from falling over each time we stand up and move around.

D.

E.

Our brain uses our eyes, ears, muscles, tendons and even touch receptors in our skin to help us balance.

F.

WHAT'S FOR DINNER?

It's time to cook a healthy, balanced meal. Read the recipe cards below and work out which one uses all the ingredients shown on the opposite page. There is a key placed at the bottom of the page to show you what the ingredients look like.

RECIPE 1

1 burger bun
4 slices of tomato
5 slices of avocado
1 bunch of coriander
1 slice of cheese
1 lettuce leaf
black beans

RECIPE 2

1 burger bun
1 bunch of coriander
mashed sweet potato
black beans
5 slices of avocado
2 slices of cheese
4 slices of tomato

Fruit and vegetables are great sources of vitamins, minerals and fibre. They are an important part of a healthy, balanced diet.

RECIPE 3

mashed sweet potato
black beans
4 lettuce leaves
4 slices of tomato
5 slices of avocado
2 slices of cheese
1 burger bun
1 bunch of coriander

Leafy green vegetables like lettuce leaves and orange vegetables such as sweet potatoes are full of vitamins. They keep you energized and support your immune system.

KEY

| BURGER BUN | TOMATO | MASHED SWEET POTATO | CORIANDER |
| CHEESE | BLACK BEANS | LETTUCE LEAVES | AVOCADO |

BLOOD COUNT CHALLENGE

There are eight blood groups (types of blood) and some
are more common than others. Look at the key below
and count up how many of each group you can find.

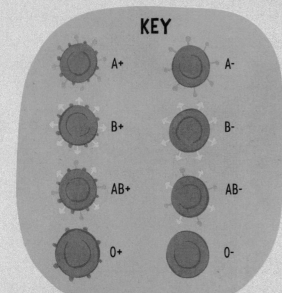

KEY

A+   A-
B+   B-
AB+ AB-
O+   O-

Every three seconds, somewhere
in the world, a person receives
a stranger's blood to help them
survive. Hospitals in the UK
alone get through an enormous
amount of blood, at the rate
of 4,000 litres a day.

Everyone's blood might look the same, but there are four main blood types, known as groups. These are called A, B, AB and O. Each group can be divided into positive and negative which means there are eight main blood groups.

Your blood group is determined by the genes that you inherit from your parents. The most common blood type in the UK is O+, followed by A+, B+ and O-.

POO PUZZLE

Your poo is created in your large and small intestines. Look at the picture below and work out which pieces fit in the empty spaces. Can you find the one that doesn't fit?

A.

B.

C.

D.

Intestines are organs that are shaped like long tubes. They help break down food so that the body can use it for energy. This is part of the process called digestion.

The average adult produces about 100 to 250 g of poo every day. That's about the weight of a large hamster!

1.

2.

3.

4.

5.

Your intestines contain tens of trillions of microbes that help break down your food.

MAKING MEMORIES

Look at the pictures below for one minute and try to remember them all. Then turn the page to test your memory power.

Your memories are not just stored in one part of the brain. A single memory can involve several parts of the brain.

A memory can be reinforced so that you remember it more clearly. Talking about the memory will attach more feelings to it, and looking at a specific photograph will also make the memory stronger.

The record for the longest sequence of objects memorized in one minute is 50. The previous record was still an impressive 45 objects.

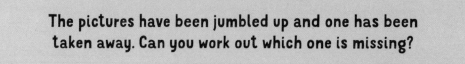

The pictures have been jumbled up and one has been taken away. Can you work out which one is missing?

FINGERPRINT MAZE

Can you find the correct way through the fingerprint?

Your fingerprints develop before you are born. Your fingerprints are made of several layers of twisted skin. These ridges of skin make patterns.

There are three different types of fingerprint patterns: loops, whorls and arches. Everyone's fingerprints are a combination of these patterns.

START

FINISH

PLAYGROUND PUZZLE

After school, this group of friends comes to the playground. This is the most active part of their day. Which tiles at the bottom of the page cannot be found in the picture?

The monkey bars are for more than just hanging around. The grasping action you need to hold on can strengthen the muscles in your arms and hands.

A.

B.

C.

D.

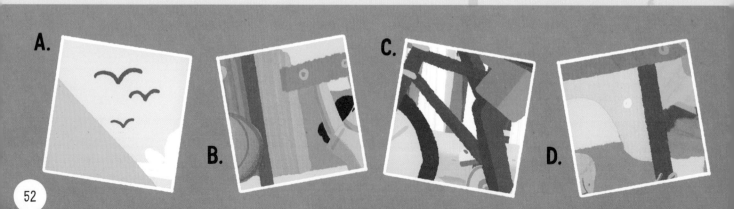

Physical changes happen to your body when you exercise. Your breathing increases to allow more oxygen to get into your bloodstream, and your heart rate goes up to get more blood to your muscles.

Exercise that works your heart is called aerobic exercise.

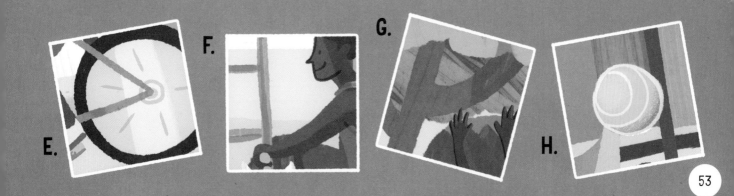

E.   F.   G.   H.

ANCIENT REMEDIES

In ancient times, some strange and scary medical procedures were carried out to try and heal people. Read the statements below and see if you can work out which are true and which are false.

CROW FEATHERS IN WOUNDS

Crow feathers are good insulators and can keep things warm. They were used by the ancient Greeks to protect wounds, like a bandage. The warmth that the feathers created meant that cuts and wounds healed much faster.

A HOLE IN THE HEAD

The act of trepanation is when a hole is drilled in a living person's head. For a large part of human prehistory, trepanation was performed to treat pain caused by skull trauma or brain diseases.

BLOOD LETTING

Leeches are bloodsucking worms. In the past, and even today, they are used by doctors. When they bite the skin, a chemical in their saliva stops blood clots forming, which can help some wounds to heal.

TOENAILS TO REPLACE ROTTEN TEETH

Toenails and teeth are made of the same substance, which made toenails a perfect replacement for rotten teeth. Dentists would bind toenails together and use tree sap to hold them in place.

BARBER SURGEONS

Imagine going to get your hair cut and the hairdresser decides to perform minor surgery on you at the same time. Up until the 19th century, hairdressers would offer services such as taking blood and pulling out teeth.

MUD BATHS

Mud baths have been used all across the world. It is believed that the minerals and nutrients in mud can help heal and soothe the skin.

EATING WORMS TO LOSE WEIGHT

Worms eat so much that they have been used to help people lose excess weight. The worms were swallowed whole so that they could feast on the food in the stomach before it was digested.

TEETH TANGLE

It's time for a trip to the dentist. Four teeth have been labelled below.
Can you match them to the correct type of tooth on the opposite page?

Young children have a set of 20 teeth, called milk teeth. From the age of about six, these teeth will fall out and are replaced by permanent teeth.

Adults can have up to 32 teeth. The last four to appear are molars right at the back of the mouth, called wisdom teeth. Not everyone gets these.

A.

B.

C.

D.

1. CANINE

There are four pointed canines that help you grip and tear food.

2. PREMOLAR

The eight premolars are flat and are used to grind and crush your food.

3. MOLAR

The 12 molars are the largest of your teeth and do a similar job to the premolars, grinding and crushing your food.

4. INCISOR

Incisors are like eight little chisels that help you slice your food.

SCHOOL SPOT

Body language is when actions and expressions are used to communicate. This classroom is full of children displaying different emotions through their body language. Can you spot 11 differences in body language between the picture below and the picture on the opposite page?

Body language can include posture, gestures, facial expressions and eye movements. Biting your nails, rubbing your hands together or scratching your head are some examples.

Folding your arms can be a way of telling people that you are feeling nervous — you are using your arms to protect yourself.

CELLS SUDOKU

Fill in the two Sudoku grids with these six types of cells. Each row, column and six-square block must only contain one of each type.

1.

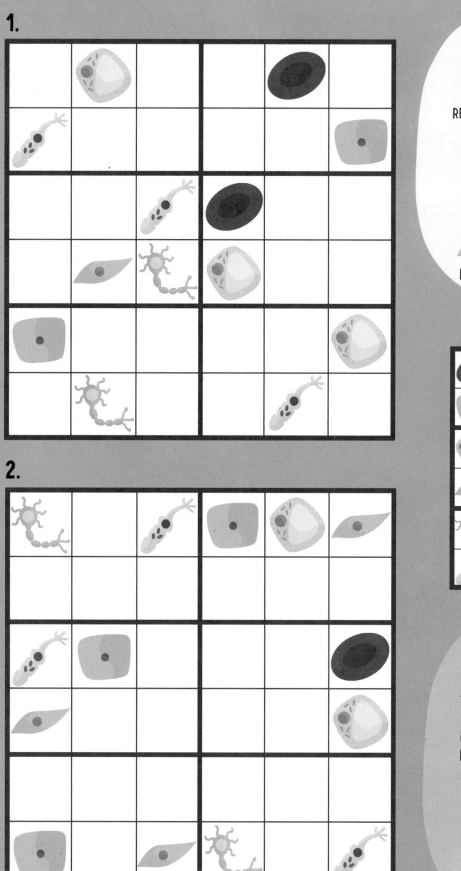

2.

CELLS

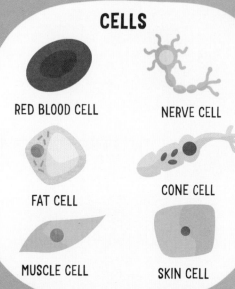

RED BLOOD CELL

NERVE CELL

FAT CELL

CONE CELL

MUSCLE CELL

SKIN CELL

EXAMPLE:

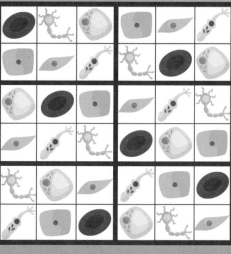

The human body is made of trillions of cells. There are about 200 different types, each with its own size, shape and contents. Each type of cell has a vital task to help the body function and stay alive. One example is nerve cells which are long and thin. They carry electrical signals to different parts of the body.

AWESOME EARS

Complete the facts about your ears by filling the gaps with the correct words from the list at the bottom of the page.

1. The innermost part of your ear is shaped like a _ _ _ _ _ .
2. The tympanic cavity, which is the middle section of your ear behind your ear drum, is only slightly larger than a _ _ _ .
3. Ears aren't only for hearing. The fluid in your inner ear also helps with _ _ _ _ _ _ _ _ _ .
4. The ear is actually made of _ _ _ _ _ parts, not just the wrinkly looking flaps on the sides of our heads.
5. Your ears are always switched on and never stop hearing sounds. Your brain just ignores most noises when you are _ _ _ _ _ _ _ _ .
6. The names for some of the parts of your ear are more like the names for things you might find in a workshop, like a _ _ _ _ _ _ and an anvil.
7. The middle ear contains three very small bones called ossicles. These ossicles are smaller than the size of a _ _ _ _ _ _ _ _ _ _ .
8. Travel sickness is caused when your _ _ _ _ _ tell your brain you are moving, but the fluid in your ears remains still. This confusion can make you feel sick.
9. _ _ _ _ contain the smallest bones in your body.
10. Your body makes ear wax to stop things like dirt and dust getting into your inner ear. This wax is actually a type of _ _ _ _ _ _ .

WORD LIST

GRAPE SEED	EYES
HAMMER	EARS
SNAIL	PEA
BALANCING	SWEAT
THREE	SLEEPING

ALVEOLUS CHALLENGE

One of these pieces doesn't fit in the picture of alveoli below. Can you examine them all and work out which one is the odd one out?

Alveoli are inside your lungs. They are little air sacs that allow oxygen to pass into your body when you breathe in and expel carbon dioxide when you breathe out.

A.

B.

C.

D.

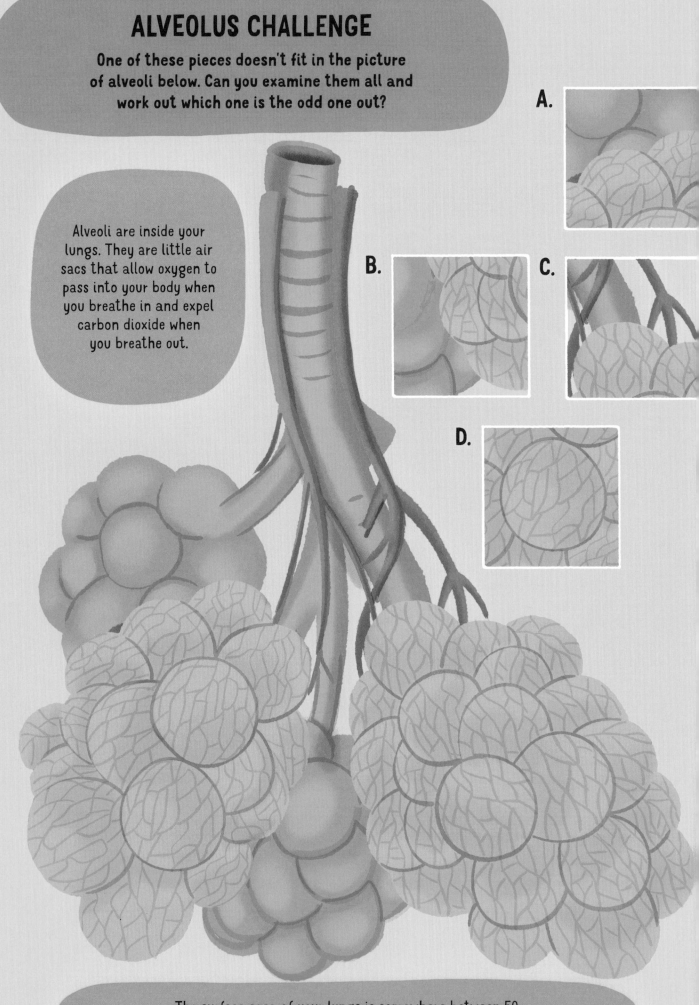

The surface area of your lungs is somewhere between 50 and 75 square metres. This means that a pair of lungs is about the same size as a tennis court.

SEEING IS BELIEVING

Optical illusions occur because your brain is trying to interpret what it sees and make sense of the world around you. Take a look at the four questions below and see what you think the answer is. Challenge your friends and family to work it out, too.

An optical illusion is a way of tricking the brain into seeing something that may not be there. Magicians use illusions all the time. In fact, magicians are sometimes referred to as illusionists.

1. Are the snakes moving in this image?

2. Are the horizontal lines sloping or straight?

3. How many legs does this elephant have?

4. Which orange circle in these two patterns is larger?

Look ahead into the distance and bring the tips of your index fingers together slowly in front of your eyes. Keep looking ahead and you'll see a floating sausage between your fingers!

MUSCLE MATHS

These heavyweight champions have got themselves in a mathematical muddle. The numbers on their T-shirts shows the total sum of the weights that they can lift. Choose the correct weights from the selection below. You can use each weight more than once.

28

WEIGHTS

12 11 5 9 4 6

EXAMPLE:

12 + 11 + 5

1. **19**

2. **14**

3.

35

4.

10

You have over 600 muscles in your body – your tongue alone has eight muscles.

5.

23

The largest muscle in the human body is in a rather surprising place ... your bottom! It is called the gluteus maximus.

Of all the muscles in your body, the muscles that control your eyes are the most active. When you are reading a book as you are now, the muscles in your eyes are moving 170 times a minute.

MEALTIME MAYHEM

Most people have three meals a day: breakfast, lunch and dinner. Can you draw three straight lines on each plate to divide it into four equal portions? Each area needs to contain one of each type of food or drink.

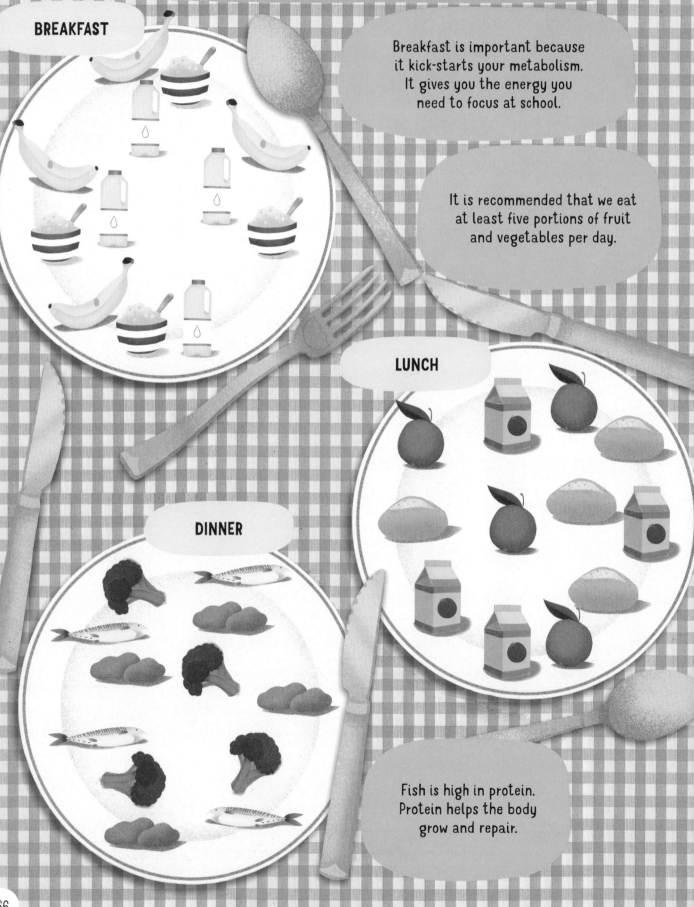

BREAKFAST

Breakfast is important because it kick-starts your metabolism. It gives you the energy you need to focus at school.

It is recommended that we eat at least five portions of fruit and vegetables per day.

LUNCH

DINNER

Fish is high in protein. Protein helps the body grow and repair.

X-RAY VISION

Can you spot the five surprising hidden objects in the X-ray below?

In a hospital, the person who operates the X-ray machine is called a radiographer.

X-rays are powerful waves of energy. They are very useful because they can go through substances that light cannot. X-rays can show images of the inside of an object, such as a human body.

Wilhelm Röntgen discovered X-rays by accident. He was experimenting with vacuum tubes when he made the discovery. He was awarded the Nobel Prize in Physics for his invention in 1901.

ALLERGIES SUDOKU

Fill in the two Sudoku grids with these six allergens. Each row,
column and six-square block must only contain one of each type.

1.

2.

ALLERGENS

ANIMAL FUR   INSECT STINGS   NUTS

POLLEN   DUST MITES   DAIRY

EXAMPLE:

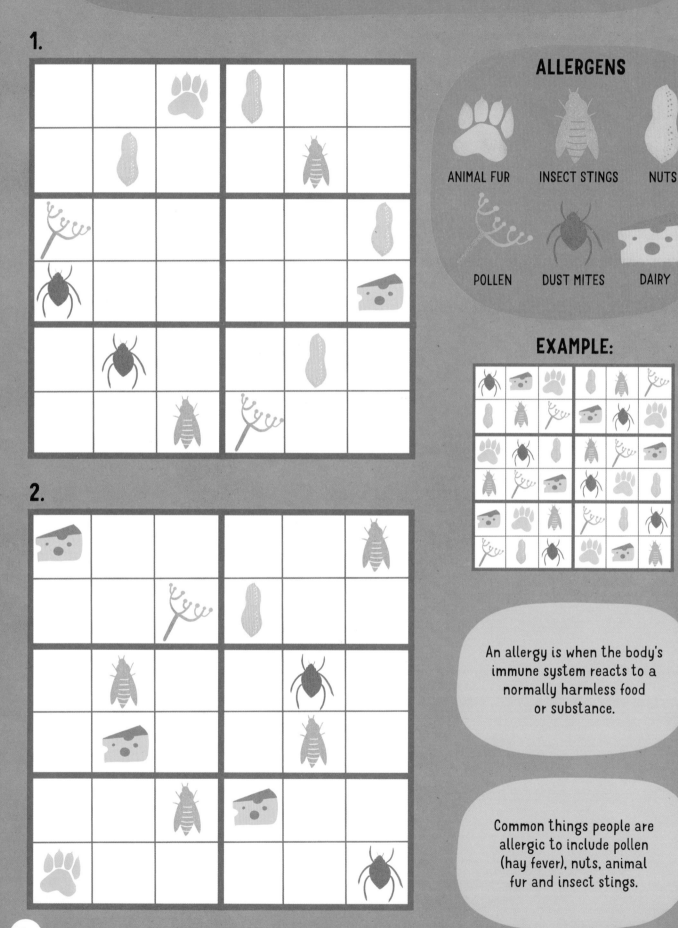

An allergy is when the body's
immune system reacts to a
normally harmless food
or substance.

Common things people are
allergic to include pollen
(hay fever), nuts, animal
fur and insect stings.

SLEEP MATCH

Everyone needs sleep, and we cannot survive without it – but we don't all need the same amount of it. Match the person to how much sleep they need by drawing a line between them and the correct clock.

NEWBORN BABY

10 HOURS

ADULT

17 HOURS

Scientists are unsure exactly why we yawn – whatever the reason, the average yawn last six seconds.

6-MONTH-OLD BABY

7 HOURS

15-YEAR-OLD

14 HOURS

We spend around a third of our lives sleeping.

8-YEAR-OLD

9 HOURS

SPOT THE SIBLING

Though some twins look identical, others can look very different from one another. Can you spot the five differences between these twins?

Identical twins don't have completely identical fingerprints. That's because fingerprints don't just depend on your genes.

Around one third of twins are identical and two thirds are non-identical.

When you look at a crowd of people, they might all look very different. However, any two people in a crowd will share 99.9 per cent of their DNA.

IQ TEST

IQ (intelligence quotient) tests measure intelligence by focusing on short-term memory, problem solving, mathematical ability and visual skills. IQ tests include puzzles which are similar to these four. Can you work out the answers?

1. Look at the sequence below and work out what comes next, either A, B or C.

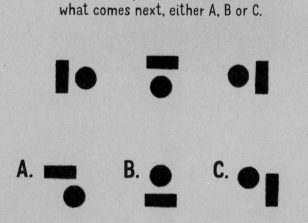

A.   B.   C.

Scientists measure intelligence on a scale called IQ. The average score is 100. A man called William James Sidis had the highest IQ score ever, somewhere between 250 and 300!

2. Here are some calculations using flowers. Can you figure out the number that each flower is worth and work out the missing answer below?

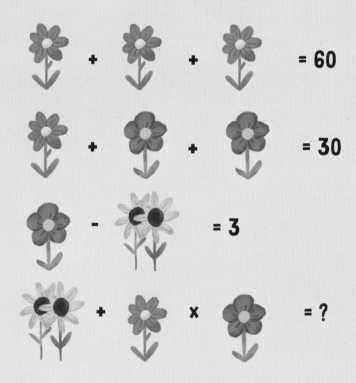

3. Can you figure out which piece below
fits the hole in the picture?

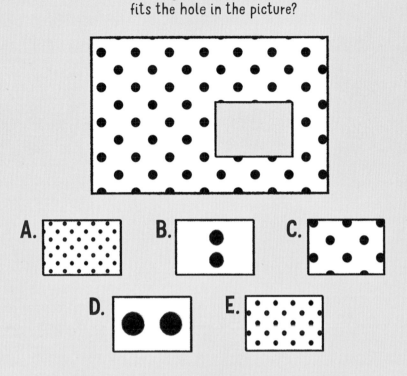

A. B. C.

D. E.

Your intelligence is a way
of telling how easy it is for
you to learn new skills and
take in knowledge.

The human brain contains
200 billion cells. Half of these
cells are neurons, which carry
signals from the brain to
the rest of the body.

4. Look at the sequence below and work out
what comes next, either A, B or C.

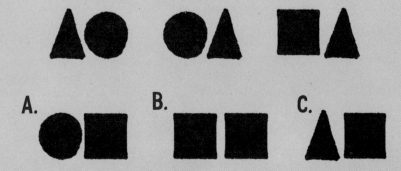

A. B. C.

MACROPHAGE MAZE

Certain white blood cells clean blood by eating old red blood cells. Take these healthy red blood cells through the maze. Don't bump into any blue macrophages!

START

Macrophages are a type of white blood cell that are part of the immune system. They eat bacteria and dead cells.

A MACROPHAGE

Your liver works really, really hard, and carries out over 500 different functions, including removing poison from your blood and storing things like fats, sugars and vitamins. It's a chemical factory!

When red blood cells break down, a substance called bilirubin is produced. This enters your intestine in bile and is what makes your poo brown.

FINISH

GOOD HYGIENE

It's important to have good hygiene as it prevents the spread of infection and can help you stay healthy in later life. Read each person's completed to-do list below and work out from the description who has done what on which day of the week. Then fill in each name on the hygiene chart on the opposite page. One name has been filled in to help you.

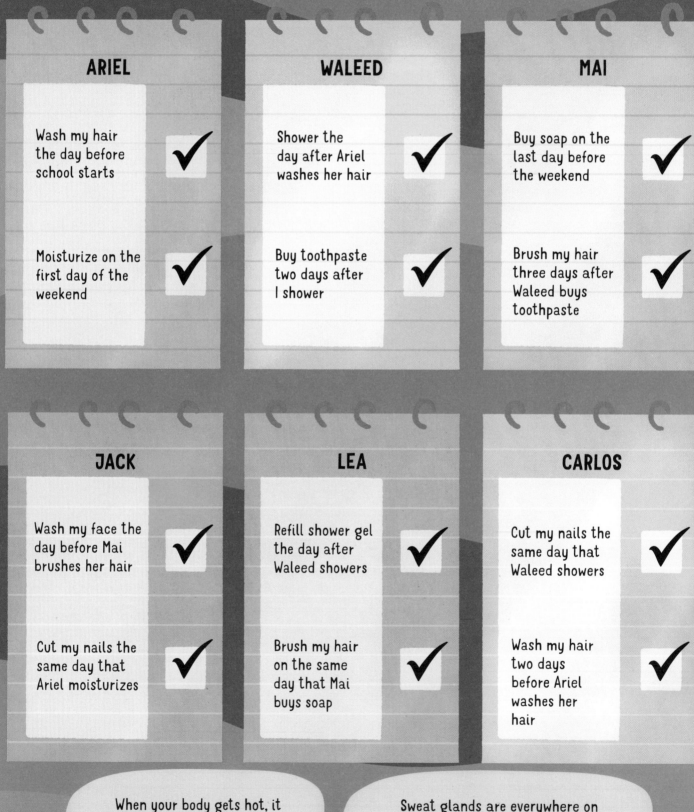

ARIEL

Wash my hair the day before school starts ✓

Moisturize on the first day of the weekend ✓

WALEED

Shower the day after Ariel washes her hair ✓

Buy toothpaste two days after I shower ✓

MAI

Buy soap on the last day before the weekend ✓

Brush my hair three days after Waleed buys toothpaste ✓

JACK

Wash my face the day before Mai brushes her hair ✓

Cut my nails the same day that Ariel moisturizes ✓

LEA

Refill shower gel the day after Waleed showers ✓

Brush my hair on the same day that Mai buys soap ✓

CARLOS

Cut my nails the same day that Waleed showers ✓

Wash my hair two days before Ariel washes her hair ✓

When your body gets hot, it produces sweat, and sweat helps bacteria grow.

Sweat glands are everywhere on your body. The average person has 2.5 million sweat glands.

HYGIENE CHART

You should wash your hands with soap regularly, to protect yourself and others from illness. Don't forget to brush your teeth twice a day.

	MONDAY	TUESDAY	WEDNESDAY	THURSDAY	FRIDAY	SATURDAY	SUNDAY
BUY SOAP							
WASHING FACE							
BUY TOOTHPASTE							
SHOWERING							
WASHING HAIR							
REFILL SHOWER GEL							
BRUSHING HAIR							
MOISTURIZING							
CUTTING NAILS	Carlos						

77

PULSE MATCHING

Your heart pushes blood through your arteries, causing them to expand and contract in response to the flow of blood. You can feel the expansions and contractions in many places throughout your body where an artery passes close to the skin. This is called a pulse and your pulse changes depending on what you are doing. Can you match the person to their pulse rate?

A.
Luke's resting pulse rate was 60 beats per minute. He then ate breakfast and it increased by 5 beats per minute.

B.
Belinda went for a run and her pulse rate was 170 beats per minute. She then stopped to stretch and it dropped by 21 beats per minute.

Depending on your age, your pulse should be somewhere between 60 and 100 beats per minute while you are resting.

C.
Suhel was on a bike ride where his pulse rate was 98 beats per minute. He stopped to take a photo and his pulse rate dropped by 13 beats per minute.

D.
Tamrin went swimming in the sea and her pulse rate jumped from 60 beats to 33 more beats per minute.

To check your heart rate, hold your palm upwards and with your other hand place your index and middle finger on your wrist below your thumb so that you can feel a throb. This is your pulse.

E.
Jonny took part in a obstacle course and his pulse rate was 124 beats per minute. When he stopped his pulse rate went down by 49 beats per minute.

F.
Marcus went to a party and danced for an hour. His pulse rate was twice his resting pulse rate of 70 beats per minute.

93

75

140

85

65

149

SIZE UP

These seven things are all found in the body. Can you work out which is the smallest and which is the largest? Label them from 1 to 7, smallest to largest, in the boxes below.

APPENDIX

BRAIN

Your appendix is a small tube that sits at the junction between the small and large intestines.

EYEBALL

STAPES (BONE)

RED BLOOD CELL

Most of the time, you won't know your appendix is there. But sometimes it can become swollen and infected – this is a condtion called appendicitis. If this happens, you may need to have an operation to remove it.

CANINE (TOOTH)

LIVER

BONUS QUESTION
How many red blood cells are there in a drop of blood?
a) 500   b) 500,000   c) 5 million

FUN AT THE FAIR

Adrenaline is a hormone in the body that gives you energy. It can be triggered when you're at a scary or exciting place, such as a theme park. Follow the directions below to navigate yourself around the theme park, then answer the questions about what you see.

DIRECTIONS

1. Start at the entrance in the bottom left-hand corner.

2. Take the left lane and walk past the log flume.

3. Follow the road round to the left where you can smell lunch cooking. Look at everyone on the ferris wheel!

4. Head south. Don't get a fright as you walk past the House of Horrors!

5. Watch out for pirates as you walk towards the hot dog stand and then take a right. Take another right and hear the soothing carousel music.

6. Take the next right and head towards the biggest ride in the theme park.

ENTRANCE

Adrenaline increases your heart rate and sends blood to your muscles so that you're ready to run away fast from anything scary.

The release of adrenaline also makes the pupil of the eye larger. This lets in more light to help us see what is happening around us as clearly as possible.

QUESTIONS

1. What rides do you visit on your route?

2. How many children are getting an ice cream?

3. How many food stalls can you see in the entire theme park?

4. What is the child by the rollercoaster holding in her hand?

5. How many trees did you go past on your route?

WHERE'S THE PAIR?

Chromosomes are the things that make us what we are. They carry all of the information used to help a cell grow, thrive and reproduce. The centre of nearly every single cell in the body contains 23 pairs of chromosomes. These pairs have been split up. Can you help them find their missing half? Both halves will be the same colour.

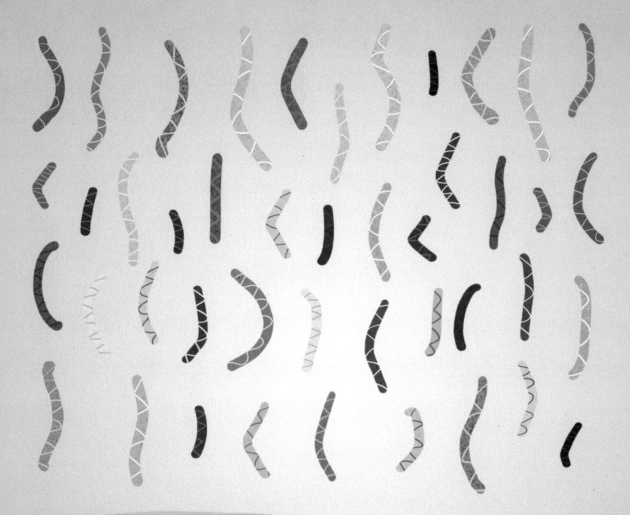

XY CHROMOSOME (MALE)   **XX CHROMOSOME (FEMALE)**

The 22 pairs above look the same in both males and females. The 23rd pair, the sex chromosomes, differs between males and females. Females have two copies of the X chromosome, while males have one X and one Y chromosome.

Each chromosome is made of a long strand of DNA. It usually looks like a piece of string, but when it is about to divide it becomes an X shape.

SKIN DETECTIVE

Look at the six statements below and see if you can figure out which are true and which are false.

1. We lose about 50,000 skin flakes a minute.

2. The skin is the human body's heaviest organ.

3. Your skin is thickest on your feet and palms.

4. Your skin makes up 32 per cent of your body weight.

5. The thinnest skin is found on your ear.

6. Your skin regenerates itself every 28 days.

ODD SENSE OUT

You have five basic senses that help you understand the world.
They tell your brain what's going on outside of your body.
Can you find the odd item out in each sense circle?

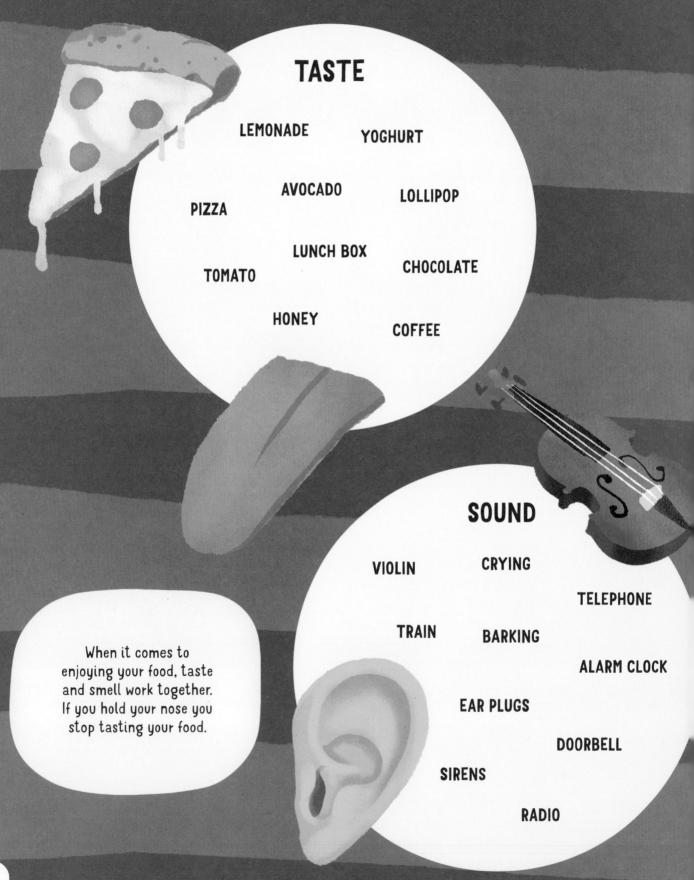

TASTE

LEMONADE   YOGHURT

AVOCADO   LOLLIPOP

PIZZA

LUNCH BOX

TOMATO   CHOCOLATE

HONEY   COFFEE

SOUND

VIOLIN   CRYING

TELEPHONE

TRAIN   BARKING

ALARM CLOCK

EAR PLUGS

DOORBELL

SIRENS

RADIO

When it comes to
enjoying your food, taste
and smell work together.
If you hold your nose you
stop tasting your food.

There are five main senses – sight, hearing, smell, touch and taste. The eyes alone contain around 70 per cent of your body's sensory receptors.

TOUCH

CACTUS

HAIR

PEN

TENNIS RACQUET

CUSHION

MOON

RUG

DOOR HANDLE

CAT

FEATHER

SIGHT

STARS

BOOK

RADIO WAVES

RAINBOW

LIGHT BULB

TELEVISION

TRAFFIC LIGHTS

OCTOPUS

MONKEY

KEYS

SMELL

SOCKS

CHEESE

FLOWER

PERFUME

LEMON

CAKE

PAIR OF GLASSES

TOOTHPASTE

SUNCREAM

ONIONS

The most sensitive parts of your skin are packed with touch receptors. Your fingertips, lips and toes are particularly sensitive.

GROUP THE GERMS

Harmful germs sometimes get into our bodies and cause diseases. Look at the key below and count up how many of each germ you can find.

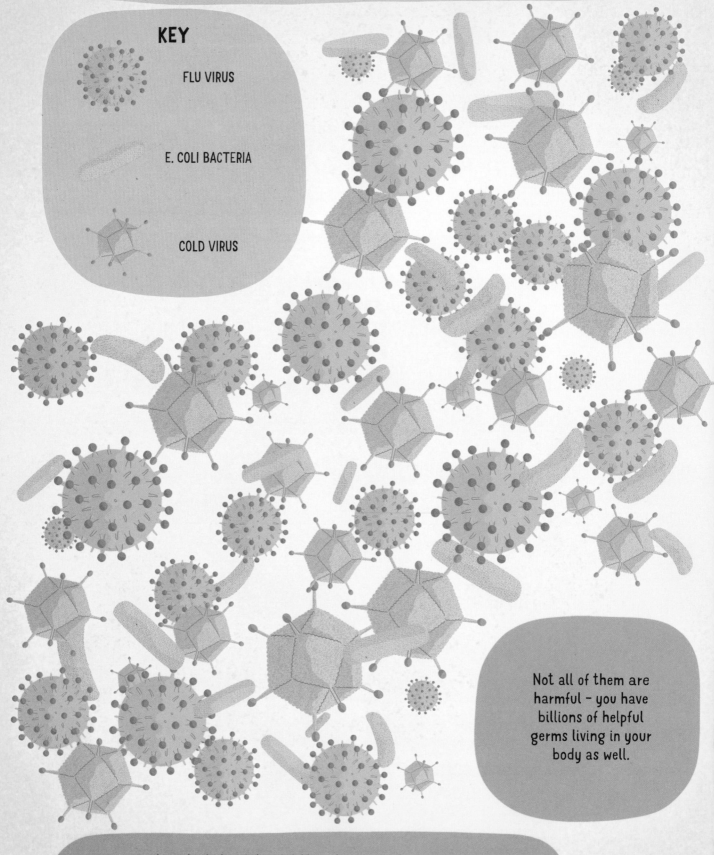

KEY

FLU VIRUS

E. COLI BACTERIA

COLD VIRUS

Not all of them are harmful – you have billions of helpful germs living in your body as well.

Your body has lots of different ways of dealing with germs to stop them attacking your body. Your skin is a barrier that can stop germs from getting in.

SKELETON DETECTIVE

Look at the six statements about bones below and see
if you can figure out which are true and which are false.

1. Your skull contains
22 bones.

2. The collarbone is one of
the most common bones
to break.

3. A dislocation is the medical
term for a broken bone.

4. Bones make up about
15 per cent of the total body
weight of an average adult.

5. Your thigh bone, also known
as your femur, is the longest
bone in your body.

6. There are 500 bones
in your body.

These four children are having a sack race at a school sports day. Follow the paths to see where each child places.

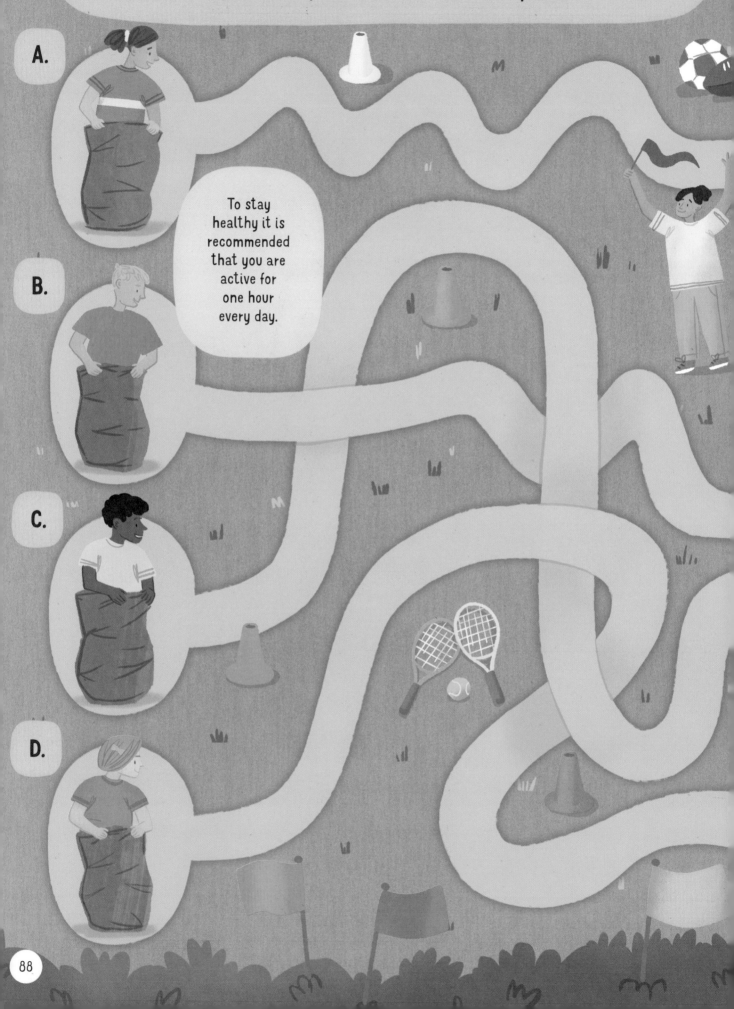

To stay healthy it is recommended that you are active for one hour every day.

We get energy from the food we eat. A calorie is the unit used to measure the amount of energy in food. When we eat and drink more calories than we use up, our bodies store the excess as body fat.

Vitamin D keeps our bones, teeth and muscles healthy. You can get your daily dose of vitamin D from being out in the sun daily for short periods with your forearms, hands or lower legs uncovered.

1ST

2ND

3RD

4TH

BRAIN-Y MAZE-Y

Can you beat the brain and complete this maze in record time? Write down how long it takes you in the space provided at the bottom of the page.

The brain is extremely sensitive and delicate, so it requires maximum protection. This is provided by the hard bone of the skull and three tough membranes called meninges.

Your brain is a fantastic organ. It enables you to think, learn, create and feel emotions, as well as controlling every blink, breath and heartbeat.

FINISH

You can challenge your brain by doing activities such as mazes, reading, playing music or anything else that gives your brain a workout.

START

Your brain is more powerful than any computer in the world. While you're awake, your brain can generate enough electricity to power a light bulb.

How long did it take you?

....

FINGER FINDING

Match each fingerprint to the correct fingertip. Can you find the fingerprint that doesn't match any fingertip? Fingerprints are flipped when pressed down so bear that in mind when matching.

No two people have the same fingerprint. Your fingerprints are completely unique.

B.

C.

A.

Fingerprints never change, even when you grow. They are a form of 'biometrics', a science that uses physical human characteristics to identify people.

1.

E.

6.

D.

G.

2.

F.

5.

3.

4.

Fingerprints help fingers and hands to grip things. The tiny ridges help to stop objects from sliding out of our hands.

TOPSY-TURVY VISION

Did you know that you actually see upside down? Your brain receives the image upside down, and then flips it round, allowing you to see things the right way up. Can you match the upside-down skeletons below to the correct skeleton on the opposite page?

Your eyes contain a small blind spot where the optic nerve passes through. Our brains use information from the other eye to fill in the vision gap so it is not noticeable.

The coloured part of your eye is called the iris. The black dot in the middle is called your pupil and is actually a hole. Light goes through this, all the way to the back of your eyeball.

PICKING BOGEYS

Bogeys are made from dried-out mucus that traps viruses, dirt, dust and pollen. Spot all the trapped items from the checklist below, and then add up your answer. Does your total match the one shown?

CHECKLIST

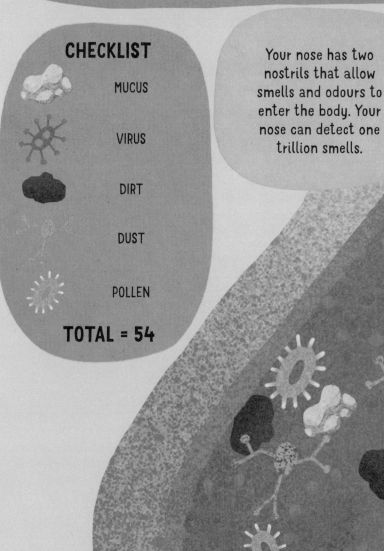

MUCUS

VIRUS

DIRT

DUST

POLLEN

TOTAL = 54

Your nose has two nostrils that allow smells and odours to enter the body. Your nose can detect one trillion smells.

Bogeys actually have a really important job. Your mucus helps to trap germs and stops them entering your body. The average nose produces around a cup of mucus each day.

You have 40 million tiny, smell-detecting hairs, called cilia, up your nose.

HEALTHY HEART

Complete the facts about your heart by filling the gaps with
the correct words from the list at the bottom of the page.

1. Your heart is about the size of your _ _ _ _ .

2. The average human heart pumps about 4-5 litres of blood per _ _ _ _ _ _ .

3. Your heart is made of two very powerful _ _ _ _ _ that work constantly to move blood around your body.

4. Blood can travel from your heart to your big toe in as little as 20 _ _ _ _ _ _ _ .

5. Your heart is a _ _ _ _ _ _ and as it contracts it sends blood around your body.

6. Blood is carried away from your heart by blood vessels called arteries and it's brought back by blood vessels called _ _ _ _ _ .

7. As blood moves through your arteries, it makes them bulge. This creates something called your _ _ _ _ _ and can be used to measure how quickly your blood is moving around your body.

8. Each half of the heart has two _ _ _ _ _ _ _ _ , a smaller upper atrium and a bigger, thicker-walled ventricle.

9. The heart beats around 2.5 billion times in an average _ _ _ _ _ _ _ _ .

10. The valves inside your heart produce a thumping sound that can be heard by something called a _ _ _ _ _ _ _ _ _ _ _ .

WORD LIST

PULSE
FIST
MINUTE
STETHOSCOPE
PUMPS
MUSCLE
VEINS
SECONDS
CHAMBERS
LIFETIME

COLOUR CONUNDRUMS

Did you know that men are much more likely to be colour blind than women? Have a go at these three colour-blind tests and see if you can work out the object in the middle.

There are three types of cells that help us see red, green and blue light. Sometimes a person might not have some of these cells, meaning they can't see certain colours. This is called colour blindness.

A.

B.

Around one in ten boys are colour blind, whereas only about one in 200 girls are colour blind.

C.

The most common form of colour blindness stops people from seeing green and red. They might find it hard to tell the difference between reds, yellows, browns and greens.

PUSH THAT BUTTON

The red button looks very appealing. Can you find the way through the maze so the neuron can pass the message to the brain that you want to press the red button?

Your neurons are special cells that carry messages to your brain in the form of electrical signals called nerve impulses.

FINISH

START

If all the neurons in your brain were lined up, they would stretch over 960 km. That's like travelling the distance from London, UK to Berlin, Germany.

Neurons communicate using electrical impulses. These impulses can travel at super speeds of 431 km per hour throughout your body. This is faster than a peregrine falcon, the fastest animal in the world.

EAT YOUR GREENS

Can you make it through these two grids to complete the games?
Follow the vegetables and fruits in the order shown in the top panel.
You can move across, up, and down but not diagonally.

1.

START

FINISH

2.

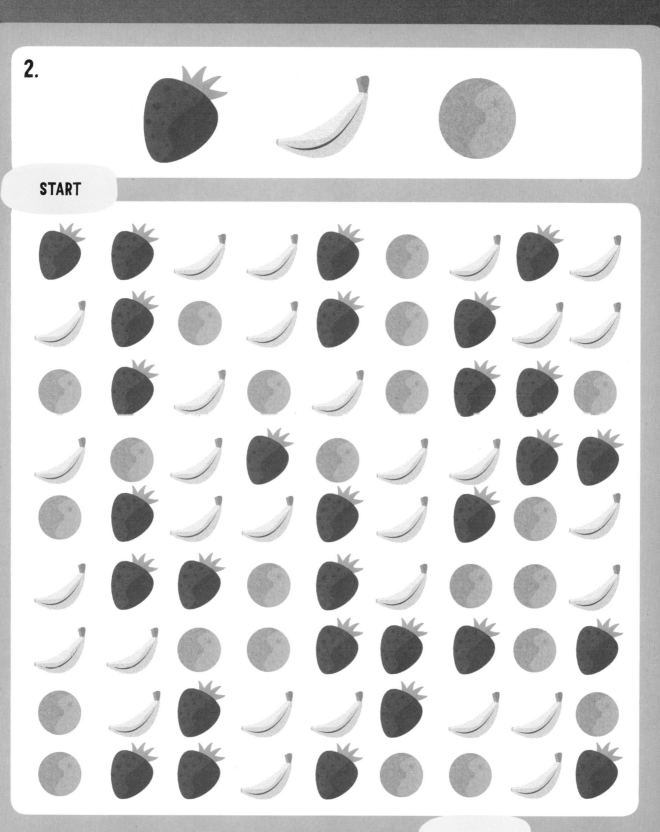

START

FINISH

Vitamin means 'vital for life'. Vitamins form an important part of nutrition and are necessary for the healthy functioning of your body.

Vitamin C is found in foods such as citrus fruit, tomatoes and Brussels sprouts. It is important for healthy skin, gums, teeth and bones.

VOMIT VORTEX

When you vomit, the muscles in your stomach and intestines push food up instead of down and carry that food right back up to your mouth. Can you help the vomit find the correct route out of the body in the maze below?

FINISH ←

When your body detects something that shouldn't be there, like bacteria or a virus, you might be sick, or vomit.

Acid is produced in your stomach to help break down your food. When you vomit, this comes up into your mouth, together with whatever you've been eating. This is partly why vomit tastes so bad!

START →

LAZY BONES

This skeleton is missing some vital bones.
Complete the dot-to-dot puzzle to fill them in.

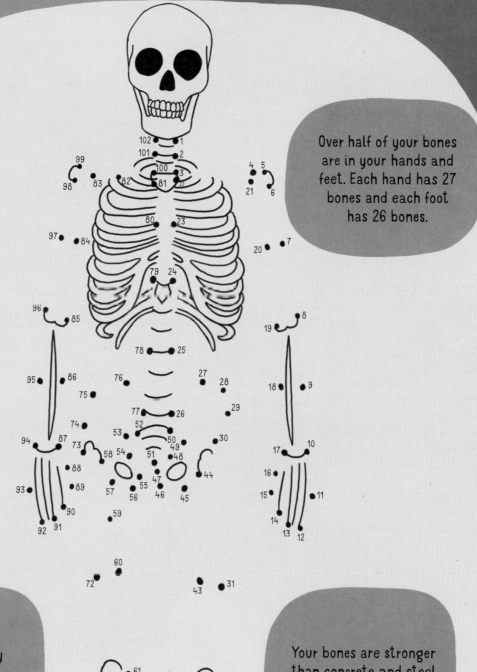

Over half of your bones
are in your hands and
feet. Each hand has 27
bones and each foot
has 26 bones.

If you break a
bone, your body
takes about 12
weeks to rebuild
the broken bone.

Your bones are stronger
than concrete and steel
but are much lighter.

THINK SMART

There are three pieces missing from the jigsaw below and there are six pieces to choose from. Can you work out which are the correct three pieces? Look at the pieces from all angles as some pieces may have been rotated.

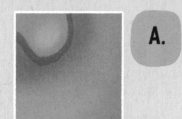

A.

1.

B.

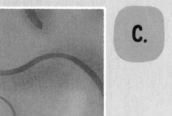

C.

Lateral thinking is a way of coming up with solutions to problems in a creative way, rather than just coming up with the obvious, logical route.

Lateral thinking can be improved through puzzles. Lateral thinking puzzles present a bit of information from which you must find an explanation. You will have to adopt creative approaches to each solution. This is how lateral thinking is developed.

2.

3.

D.

E.

F.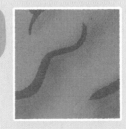

Scientists believe that the largest part of the brain, which is called the cerebrum, controls logic and creativity.

THE CELL FACTORY

Each of these cells have a different job. Follow the tangled lines to work out where each cell needs to get to.

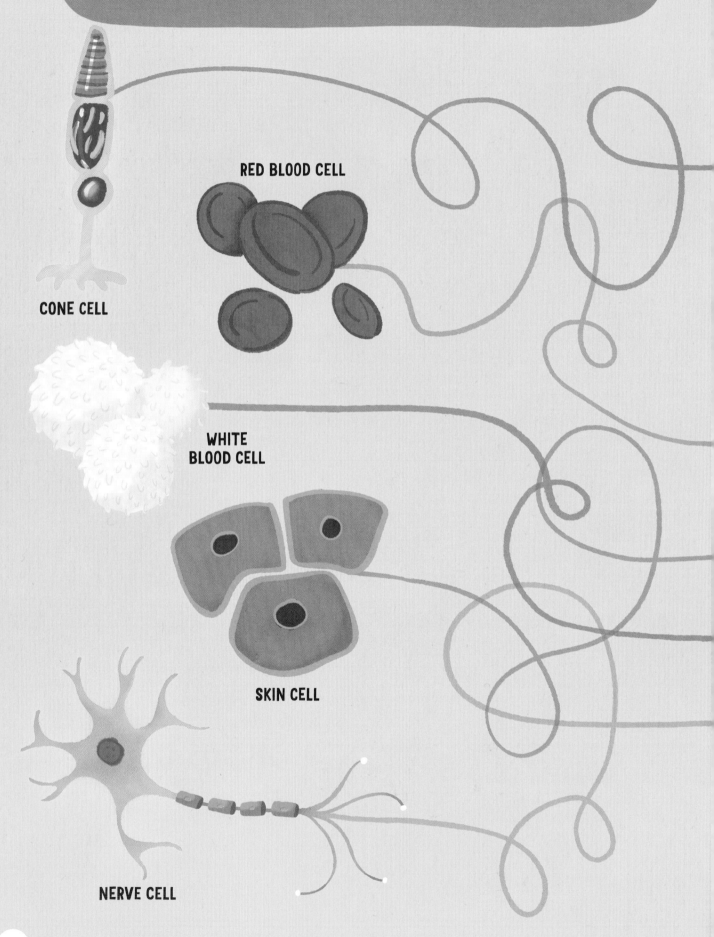

CONE CELL

RED BLOOD CELL

WHITE BLOOD CELL

SKIN CELL

NERVE CELL

The human body is made up of tiny living blocks called cells. There are around 30 trillion cells in the human body.

BRAIN
These cells carry electrical signals in the nervous system.

EYE
These cells respond to light so you can see colour.

HAND
These cells form a protective layer that covers the body.

LUNGS
These cells carry oxygen from the lungs around the body.

Red blood cells are some of the smallest cells in the human body. They are so small that nearly 30 billion of them would fit in a teaspoon.

WOUND
These cells help to fight off infection.

SKELETON SEARCH

Can you draw lines between the bones on the right-hand page and the skeleton below to show where each bone is found in the body?

A baby is born with more bones in its body than an adult. We start with 270 soft bones that eventually fuse together, leaving us with 206 bones as we get older.

Your spine runs all the way down your back and protects the delicate spinal cord.

The stapes is a little bone in your ear and, as well as helping you hear, it is the smallest bone in your body.

SCAPULA

TAILBONE

MANDIBLE

SPINE

HUMERUS

FEMUR

LEARN ABOUT LUNGS

Complete the facts about your lungs by filling the gaps with
the correct words from the list at the bottom of the page.

1. Every cell in your body needs _ _ _ _ _ _ to function.
2. Lungs are the only human organs that can _ _ _ _ _ on water.
3. You breathe in air that contains oxygen (among other things), and you
   breathe out _ _ _ _ _ _ _ _ _ _ _ _ _ .
4. Even when we breathe out, our lungs always retain _ _ _ litre of air in the airways.
5. Your lungs process around 8,000–9,000 litres of air every _ _ _ .
6. Your diaphragm is a domed sheet of _ _ _ _ _ _ that helps your
   lungs shrink and expand.
7. Your lungs are protected by your _ _ _ _ _ _ _ .
8. Lungs are part of the _ _ _ _ _ _ _ _ _ _ _ system.
9. In the lungs, oxygen passes from the alveoli into
   the _ _ _ _ _ _ _ _ _ _ _ in exchange for carbon dioxide.
10. _ _ _ _ _ _ is a type of mucus that is produced in the lungs.

WORD LIST

PHLEGM
DAY
FLOAT
ONE
CARBON DIOXIDE
MUSCLE
RIBCAGE
RESPIRATORY
BLOODSTREAM
OXYGEN

FUNNY BONES

Did you know that you have 27 bones in your hand? Circle the picture below that includes all of the bones that make up this hand.

The fingers and thumb on each hand are made up of 14 bones, called phalanges.

The large number of bones, muscles and tendons found in our hands mean that we can carry out lots of different functions, from lifting heavy objects to more delicate jobs like threading a needle.

A.

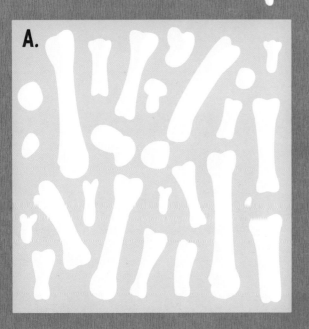

B.

C.

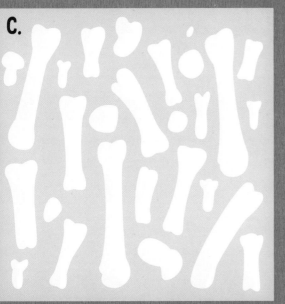

D.

TASTE TEST BINGO

This kitchen is full of sweet, salty, sour, bitter and umami (savoury) things to eat and drink. Search the kitchen for all of the items pictured on the bingo cards on the opposite page. Time yourself to see how quickly you can find them or challenge a friend to a race.

SWEETS	PEACHES	LEMONS
YOGHURT	SOY SAUCE	PIZZA
COFFEE	CRANBERRY JUICE	MUSHROOMS

Umami describes strong, savoury flavours in things like cheese, meat and fish. It was first scientifically identified at Tokyo Imperial University in 1908.

Your tongue can only actually taste whether a food is sweet, sour, salty, bitter or savoury (umami) when your saliva starts to dissolve the food. Messages are sent to the brain, together with smell information, to identify flavours.

APRICOT JAM	BALSAMIC VINEGAR	LIME
BACON	OLIVES	BRUSSELS SPROUTS
ORANGE	CHEESE	TOMATOES

Each person has between 5,000 and 10,000 taste buds, most of which are on the upper surface of the tongue. There are also taste buds across the roof of the mouth and in the throat.

PARTY TIME

Our faces can show others how we are feeling. The children at this birthday party are feeling a range of emotions. Can you spot the ten differences between the picture below and the picture on the opposite page?

We are able to express six basic emotions using our faces without saying a word. These are happiness, sadness, fear, surprise, anger and disgust.

It is possible to experience more than one emotion at the same time. One example is that you can be both happy and scared about the first day at a new school.

THE BIG HUMAN BODY QUIZ

1. What does the left side of the brain control?

A. Logic
B. Creativity
C. Emotions

2. What is the largest muscle in the human body?

A. Biceps (arms)
B. Gluteus maximus (bottom)
C. Quadriceps (legs)

3. How many bones are there in an adult human body?

A. 700
B. 520
C. 206

4. Which cells help you to see colour in bright light?

A. Cone cells
B. Rod cells
C. Nerve cells

5. What taste is umami?

A. Savoury
B. Sweet
C. Sour

6. Which of the following is not a good source of calcium?

A. Milk
B. Cheese
C. Carrots

7. What percentage of your body is made up of water?

A. 60 per cent
B. 45 per cent
C. 20 per cent

8. Which is the heaviest internal organ in the human body?

A. Liver
B. Stomach
C. Lung

9. Which of the following is not a blood type?

A. A+
B. B+
C. D-

10. How many milk teeth do young children have?

A. 28
B. 20
C. 32

11. What are chromosomes made of?

A. DNA
B. Carbon dioxide
C. Bone marrow

12. What is the name of the unit used to measure noise?

A. Decibels
B. Kilograms
C. Kelvin

13. Which of the following is not an example of a reflex action?

A. Blinking
B. Sneezing
C. Walking

14. What is the average number of breaths the human body takes every day?

A. 20,000
B. 12,000
C. 52,000

15. How many main senses are there in the human body?

A. Seven
B. Five
C. Two

ALL THE ANSWERS

JOINING JOINTS P4–5

A – 3 (Knuckles)
B – 6 (Knee)
C – 7 (Hip)
D – 4 (Shoulder)
E – 5 (Wrist)
F – 2 (Elbow)
G – 1 (Ankle)

BACTERIA HUNT P6

21 green bacteria are hiding in the scene.

SUPERHUMAN BODY PARTS P7

Group B contains all the correct parts.

SUPERMARKET SWEEP P8–9

There are 28 items.

5 milk
5 bananas
6 apples
7 oranges
5 carrots

DECIBEL DISCOVERY P10–11

A pin dropping – 10 decibels
A thunderstorm – 120 decibels
An aeroplane taking off – 140 decibels
An alarm clock – 80 decibels
A rocket launch – 180 decibels
A vacuum cleaner – 75 decibels
A balloon popping – 125 decibels

MEDICAL MEMORY MUDDLE P12–15

The DNA is facing the other way.

WHO POOED? P18–19

Lily did the poo.

ANIMAL SIBLINGS P20–21

1. True
2. False
3. True
4. True
5. False
6. True
7. True
8. True

GROWING UP P22–23

1. Nathan is 148 cm
2. Kamal is 138 cm
3. Ava is 143 cm
4. Vihaan is 147 cm
5. Anna is 137 cm
6. Marie is 139 cm

SMELLY BINGO P24–25

STAYING HYDRATED P30–31

1,000 ml ÷ 2 ml = 500 ml
657 ml + 343 ml = 1,000 ml
175 ml - 25 ml = 150 ml
170 ml + 180 ml = 350 ml
Total: 2,000 ml

HEAD SCRATCHING P32–33

14 head lice
17 nits

BODY-CLOCK CONUNDRUM P34–35

A (18:30) – **5** (Blood pressure begins to drop)
B (22:30) – **3** (Least likely to need a poo)
C (03:00) – **8** (Lowest body temperature)
D (08:30) – **1** (Most likely to need a poo)
E (11:00) – **4** (Brain fully alert and active)
F (14:30) – **7** (Best coordination)
G (02:00) – **6** (Deepest stage of sleep)
H (16:00) – **2** (Best time for sport)

PICKING SIDES P26–27

Left side	Right side
Language	Imagination
Writing	Music
Puzzles	Spatial awareness
Maths and science	Art

TOUCH RECEPTORS P38

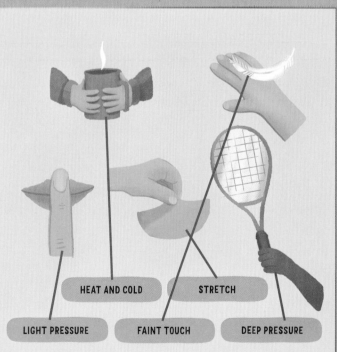

SHADOWY SILHOUETTES P28–29

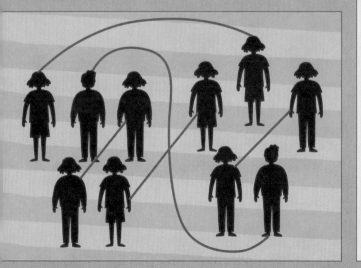

SOLVE THE SUPER SEQUENCE P39

A. 11 14 17 20 **23** (add 3 each time)
B. 2 4 8 16 **32** (multiply previous number by 2)
C. 17 19 23 29 **37** (add 2, 4, 6, 8 and so on)

BODY SWAP P40–41

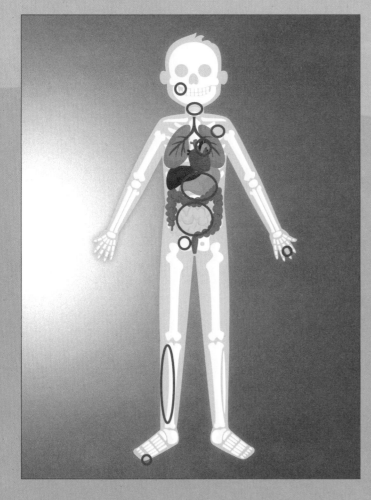

WALK THE LINE P42–43

1 is trying to reach **D**
2 is trying to reach **C**
3 is trying to reach **B**
4 is trying to reach **A**
5 is trying to reach **F**
6 is trying to reach **E**

WHAT'S FOR DINNER? P44–45

Recipe 3 contains the correct ingredients.

BLOOD COUNT P46–47

A+	5
A-	10
B+	7
B-	8
AB+	4
AB-	6
O+	11
O-	9

POO PUZZLE P48

Piece **1** is the odd one out
A – 2
B – 5
C – 4
D – 3

MAKING MEMORIES P49–50

The **camera** is missing.

FINGERPRINT MAZE P51

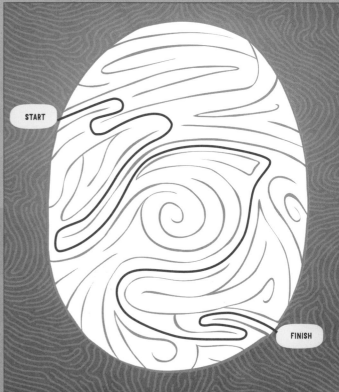

PLAYGROUND PUZZLE P52–53

Images **A**, **C** and **H** do not appear in the scene.

ANCIENT REMEDIES P54–55

Crow feathers in wounds is **false**
A hole in the head is **true**
Blood letting is **true**
Toenails to replace rotten teeth is **false**
Barber surgeons is **true**
Mud baths is **true**
Eating worms to lose weight is **false**

TEETH TANGLE P56–57

A – 4
B – 3
C – 2
D – 1

SCHOOL SPOT P58–59

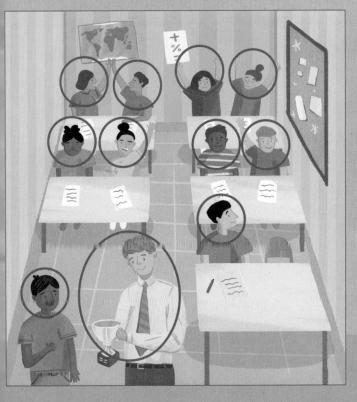

CELLS SUDOKU P60

1.

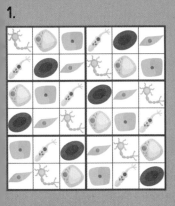

2.

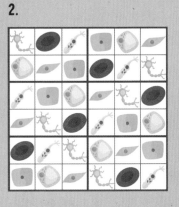

AWESOME EARS P61

1. The innermost part of your ear is shaped like a **SNAIL**.
2. The tympanic cavity, which is the middle section of your ear behind your ear drum, is only slightly larger than a **PEA**.
3. Ears aren't only for hearing. The fluid in your inner ear also helps with **BALANCING**.
4. The ear is actually made of **THREE** parts, not just the wrinkly looking flaps on the sides of our heads.
5. Your ears are always switched on and never stop hearing sounds. Your brain just ignores most noises when you are **SLEEPING**.
6. The names for some of the parts of your ear are more like the names for things you might find in a workshop, like a **HAMMER** and an anvil.
7. The middle ear contains three very small bones called ossicles. These ossicles are smaller than the size of a **GRAPE SEED**.
8. Travel sickness is caused when your **EYES** tell your brain you are moving, but the fluid in your ears remains still. This confusion can make you feel sick.
9. **EARS** contain the smallest bones in your body.
10. Your body makes ear wax to stop things like dirt and dust getting into your inner ear. This wax is actually a type of **SWEAT**.

ALVEOLUS CHALLENGE P62

The odd one out is **B**.

SEEING IS BELIEVING P63

1. The snakes are **not** moving.
2. All of the lines are **straight**. The black and white blocks are not aligned and so fool your brain into thinking that the lines are sloping.
3. **Four**
4. The orange circles are the **same size**. Your brain can be influenced or tricked by the scale and closeness of other objects to the object being judged.

MUSCLE MATHS P64–65

1. 19 = 4 + 6 + 9
2. 14 = 5 + 9
3. 35 = 4 + 5 + 6 + 9 + 11
4. 10 = 4 + 6
5. 23 = 12 + 11

MEALTIME MAYHEM P66

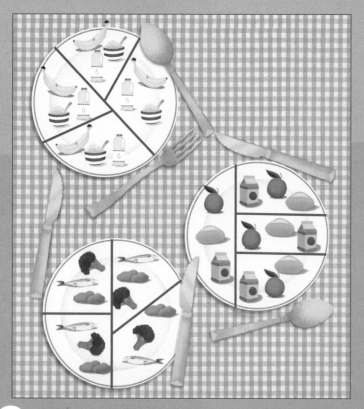

X-RAY VISION P67

The hidden objects are a **key**, a **marble**, a **coin**, a **ring** and a **piece of Lego**.

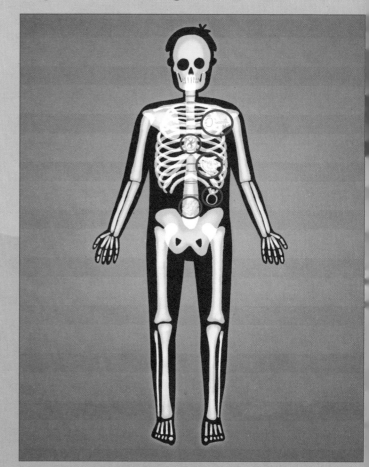

ALLERGIES SUDOKU P68

1.

2.

SLEEP MATCH P69

Newborn baby – **17 hours**
Adult – **7 hours**
6-month-old baby – **14 hours**
15-year-old – **9 hours**
8-year-old – **10 hours**

SPOT THE SIBLING P70–71

Differences:
Hair colour
Curly hair
Freckles
Eye colour
Gap between teeth

IQ TEST P72–73

1. **B.** It is moving round clockwise.
2. Pink flower = **20**
   Purple flower = **5**
   Yellow flower = **2**
   Answer = 110
3. **Piece C** fits in the picture. It has the same density of spots.
4. **C.** The pairs of patterns reflect each other.

MACROPHAGE MAZE P74–75

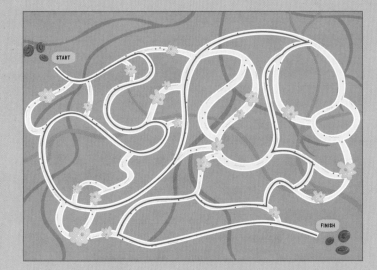

GOOD HYGIENE P76–77

	MONDAY	TUESDAY	WEDNESDAY	THURSDAY	FRIDAY	SATURDAY	SUNDAY
BUY SOAP					Mai		
WASHING FACE					Jack		
BUY TOOTHPASTE			Waleed				
SHOWERING	Waleed						
WASHING HAIR					Carlos		Ariel
REFILL SHOWER GEL		Lea					
BRUSHING HAIR					Lea	Mai	
MOISTURIZING						Ariel	
CUTTING NAILS	Carlos					Jack	

PULSE MATCHING P78

A – 65
B – 149
C – 85
D – 93
E – 75
F – 140

SIZE UP P79

From smallest to largest:
1 – Red blood cell
2 – Stapes (bone)
3 – Appendix
4 – Canine (tooth)
5 – Eyeball
6 – Brain
7 – Liver
Bonus question: **C.** There are five million red blood cells in a single drop of blood.

FUN AT THE FAIR P80–81

1. Log flume, ferris wheel, haunted house, pirate ship, carousel, rollercoaster
2. Five children
3. Four
4. Balloon
5. Ten trees

CHROMOSOME MATCH P82

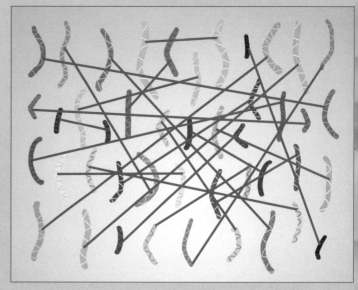

SKIN DETECTIVE P83

1. True
2. True
3. True
4. False
5. False
6. True

ODD SENSE OUT P84–85

Taste – Lunch box
Sound – Ear plugs
Sight – Radio waves
Touch – Moon
Smell – Pair of glasses

GROUP THE GERMS P86

25 flu virus
26 E. coli bacteria
23 cold virus

SKELETON DETECTIVE P87

1. True
2. True
3. False
4. True
5. True
6. False

SCHOOL SPORTS RACE P88–89

A came 4th
B came 2nd
C came 1st
D came 3rd

BRAIN-Y MAZE-Y P90

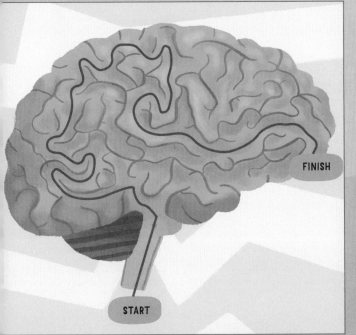

FINISH

START

FINGER FINDING P91

A – 2
B – 1
C – 3
D – 4
E is the odd one out.
F – 5
G – 6

TOPSY-TURVY VISION P92–93

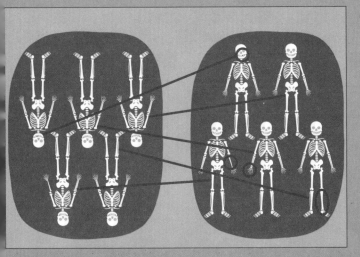

PICKING BOGEYS P94

12 mucus
11 virus
6   dirt
13 dust
12 pollen

HEALTHY HEART P95

1. Your heart is about the size of your **FIST**.
2. The average human heart pumps about 4-5 litres of blood per **MINUTE**.
3. Your heart is made of two very powerful **PUMPS** that work constantly to move blood around your body.
4. Blood can travel from your heart to your big toe in as little as 20 **SECONDS**.
5. Your heart is a **MUSCLE** and as it contracts it sends blood around your body.
6. Blood is carried away from your heart by blood vessels called arteries and it's brought back by blood vessels called **VEINS**.
7. As blood moves through your arteries, it makes them bulge. This creates something called your **PULSE** and can be used to measure how quickly your blood is moving around your body.
8. Each half of the heart has two **CHAMBERS**, a smaller upper atrium and a bigger, thicker-walled ventricle.
9. The heart beats around 2.5 billion times in an average **LIFETIME**.
10. The valves inside your heart produce a thumping sound that can be heard by something called a **STETHOSCOPE**.

COLOUR CONUNDRUMS P96

A. A rabbit
B. The number 29
C. A star

PUSH THAT BUTTON P97

FINISH

START

EAT YOUR GREENS P98-99

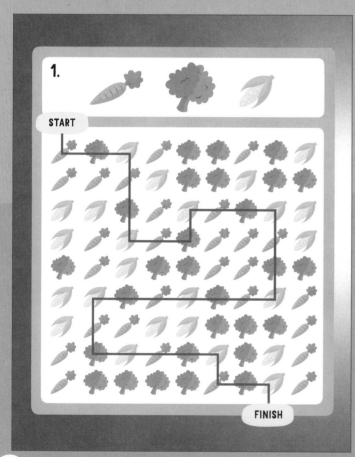

1.

START

FINISH

VOMIT VORTEX P100

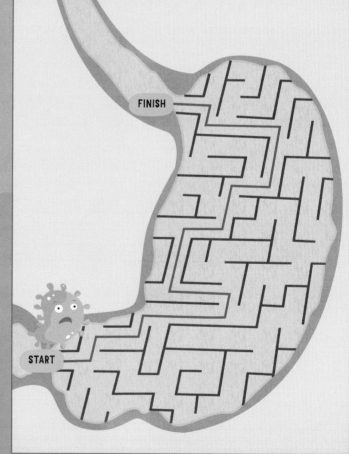

FINISH

START

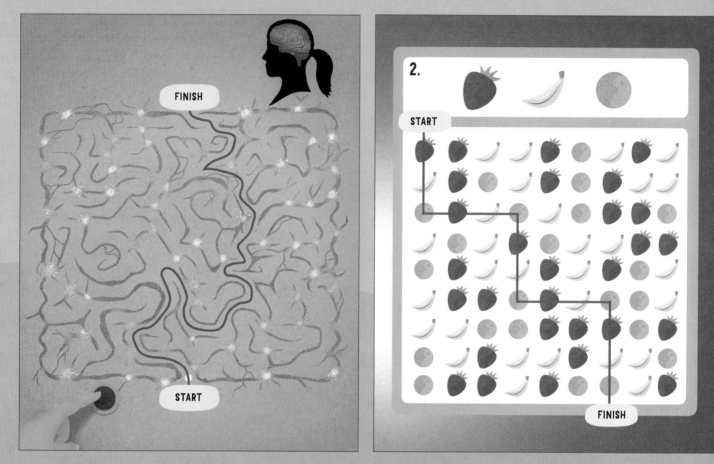

2.

START

FINISH

LAZY BONES P101

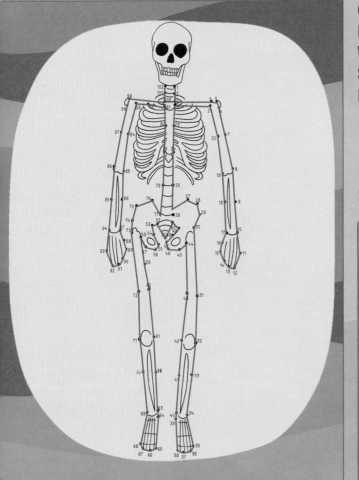

THE CELL FACTORY P104–105

Cone cell – Eye
Red blood cell – Lungs
White blood cell – Wound
Skin cell – Hand
Nerve cell – Brain

SKELETON SEARCH P106–107

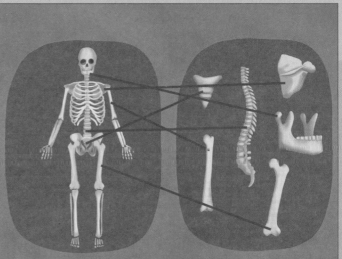

THINK SMART P102–103

Piece **D** fits in space **1**
Piece **C** fits in space **2**
Piece **E** fits in space **3**

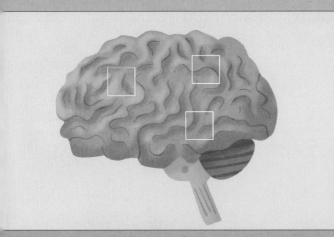

LEARN ABOUT LUNGS P108

1. Every cell in your body needs **OXYGEN** to function.
2. Lungs are the only human organs that can **FLOAT** on water.
3. You breathe in air that contains oxygen (among other things), and you breathe out **CARBON DIOXIDE**.
4. Even when we breathe out, our lungs always retain **ONE** litre of air in the airways.
5. Your lungs process around 8,000–9,000 litres of air every **DAY**.
6. Your diaphragm is a domed sheet of **MUSCLE** that helps your lungs shrink and expand.
7. Your lungs are protected by your **RIBCAGE**.
8. Lungs are part of the **RESPIRATORY** system.
9. In the lungs, oxygen passes from the alveoli into the **BLOODSTREAM** in exchange for carbon dioxide.
10. **PHLEGM** is a type of mucus that is produced in the lungs.

FUNNY BONES P109

Group C contains all the correct parts.

PARTY TIME P112–113

TASTE TEST BINGO P110–111

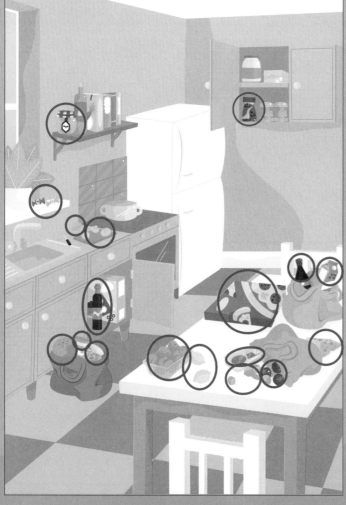

THE BIG HUMAN BODY QUIZ P114–115

1. A – Logic
2. B – Gluteus maximus (bottom)
3. C – 206
4. A – Cone cells
5. A – Savoury
6. C – Carrots
7. A – 60 per cent
8. A – Liver
9. C – D-
10. B – 20
11. A – DNA
12. A – Decibels
13. C – Walking
14. A – 20,000
15. B – Five

GLOSSARY

Adrenaline
A hormone in the body that gives you energy in times of danger or excitement.

Allergen
A normally harmless substance that is capable of triggering a reaction from your body's immune system.

Allergy
When your body's immune system reacts to a food or substance that is normally harmless.

Alveolus (plural: Alveoli)
One of the little air sacs inside your lungs that allow oxygen to pass into your body and carbon dioxide to be expelled.

Artery
A blood vessel that carries blood away from your heart to your body's organs and tissues.

Bacterium (plural: Bacteria)
A small microorganism.

Bilirubin
A substance that is produced when red blood cells break down. It is what makes your poo brown.

Biometrics
Science that uses human characteristics to identify people.

Blood vessel
Any tube that carries blood through your body.

Calorie
The unit used to measure the amount of energy in food.

Cell
The smallest living part of your body.

Cerebrum
The largest part of the brain, understood to control logic and creativity.

Chromosome
A strand of DNA found in your body's cells.

Cilia
Tiny hairs in your nose.

Constipation
When you are unable to poo.

Decibel
The unit used to measure sound.

Dehydration
When there is not enough water in your body.

Digestion
The process that breaks your food down so it is small enough for your body to absorb and use.

Genes
Instructions that control the way your body works and develops. They are passed on from parents to their children.

Head louse (plural: Head lice)
A tiny insect that lives on human hair. See also: Nits.

Heart rate
The rate at which your heart beats.

Hormone
A chemical produced by your body to change the way different parts of your body work.

Immune system
A collection of cells and tissues that protect the body from disease.

IQ (Intelligence quotient)
The scale on which intelligence is measured.

Macrophage
A type of white blood cell that eats bacteria and dead cells.

Meninges
The three tough membranes that protect the brain and the spinal cord.

Metabolism
The way chemical processes in your body cause food to be used efficiently, such as making new cells and giving you energy.

Minerals
A natural chemical that is needed in your diet to keep your body healthy.

Nerve impulse
An electrical signal carried around your body by neurons.

Nervous system
A special system of nerve cells that controls the body.

Neuron
Also known as a nerve cell. These carry information around your body as electrical signals, known as nerve impulses.

Nits
The empty egg shells that head lice have hatched from. See also: **Head louse**.

Nutrients
Basic chemicals that are found in food that your body uses for fuel, growth and repair.

Optic nerve
Connects the eye to the brain and transfers visual information.

Organ
A body part that has a particular function, such as your heart or your brain.

Ossicle
A very small bone, specifically the three small bones inside the tympanic cavity of the ear.

Phalange
The small length of bone in between one knuckle and the next on your hands.

Prosthetic
An artificial replacement for a body part.

Pupil
The black hole in the middle of your eye, through which light enters.

Radiographer
A person who operates an X-ray machine.

Reflex
A quick, automatic response, such as blinking or moving your hand away from something hot.

Spatial awareness
Knowing where your body is in relation to other objects and people.

Spinal cord
A collection of nerve cells that runs down your spine and connects your brain to the rest of your body.

Synovial joint
A joint that is able to move.

Tendon
Tough connective tissue that links muscles to bones.

Tympanic cavity
The middle section of your ear behind your ear drum.

Umami
The word used to describe a strong, savoury flavour.

Virus
A type of germ that invades cells. Viruses cause common colds, measles and flu.

Vitamin
A substance that is needed in your diet to keep your body healthy.

X-ray
A form of radiation that can be used on humans to see bones.